The
Five
PRINCIPLES

The Five PRINCIPLES

A Guide to Practical Spirituality

Ellen Debenport

The Five Principles

First edition 2009

To place an order, call the Customer Service department at 1-800-669-0282 or go online at *www.unity.org.*

The publisher wishes to acknowledge the editorial work of Toni M. Lapp; the copy services of Dan Rebant, Lila Herrmann and Peter Harakas; the marketing efforts of Adrianne Ford; and the project management of Sharon Sartin and Julie Boles.

Cover design by Karen Rizzo
Interior design by Karen Rizzo
Library of Congress Control Number: 2008942363
ISBN: 978-0-87159-330-6
Canada BN 13252 0933 RT

Table of Contents

Introduction

A principle is a rule or law that never changes. It applies to all people, everywhere, all the time.

We learned this as children. Two plus two equals four, anywhere, all the time. It's a mathematical principle. If you get an answer other than four, the mistake is yours, not the principle's. Your answer never depends on your good or bad behavior; the principle is not even aware of you. It just *is*. Two plus two will always be four, for you and everyone else.

Spiritual principles work the same way. They are laws of the universe that govern all people, all the time. We can learn how to use them to great advantage, like mathematical principles, or we can ignore them and continually get answers that don't work for us.

Suppose you didn't understand the law of gravity, didn't have a name for it or know what was happening.

You might wonder, *Why do my feet stick to the ground? I can lift them, but it takes effort. The faster I try to move, the more tired I get. Why do I fall down if I step off a cliff? Why does an object drop to the ground when I release it? Why doesn't it float? Why don't I float? Am I being punished? Have I displeased God in some way? I should pray harder and have more faith!*

Such a person would be laughable—ignorant of the way the world works and needlessly frustrated by life. Once we know that gravity will always pull things toward the ground, we can work within it, adjust for it. Despite gravity, we build ever-taller skyscrapers and fly ever farther into space. The principle of gravity does not limit us but gives us parameters to work within. And it is constant, at least on the earth plane. What a relief that gravity is not arbitrarily stronger or weaker from day to day and does not change its strength in different spots on Earth. It never holds on to some people while letting others drift away, depending on how much it loves them.

Spiritual principles are the same—constant, unchanging, impersonal. They work with or without our understanding and hold no opinion of our behavior. What a relief it would be to understand what they are and how we can work within them.

That is the purpose of this book. The Five Principles were first written in this specific form for the Unity spiritual movement, but they reflect laws of the universe. The laws apply to everyone, all the time.

The Unity movement claims no corner on spiritual truth; these principles show up in every major religion. The Earth's great spiritual teachers—Buddha, Jesus, many others—taught these laws. The principles have been tested throughout human history, discovered and rediscovered by spiritual seekers. Like mathematicians, spiritual students have learned by trial and error, experiment and research, that these laws work the same way, every time, for everyone.

Unity was founded in 1889 by Charles and Myrtle Fillmore in Kansas City, Missouri. Because Unity has a Christian base, this book reflects Christianity, the Bible and Jesus as a model for spiritual living. But the Fillmores, who began exploring metaphysics as a means of healing themselves physically, drew ideas from all the world's religions, found what worked for them, and shared it through their publications, prayer and teaching. They also saw the principles clearly revealed in the words of Jesus. Some of his teachings that reflect these Five Principles are included at the beginning of each chapter.

A century later, the Fillmores' great-granddaughter Connie Fillmore Bazzy, an ordained Unity minister and then president of Unity School of Christianity, was asked to summarize Unity's teachings in an article for *Daily Word*® magazine. This article was later incorporated into a booklet titled *The Keys to the Kingdom: Five Fundamentals of Truth*, published in 1990 to be used as a month-long study of Unity principles. She condensed the teachings of Unity into five essential points.

"My basis for the way that I framed it was out of what I had studied in ministerial school," said Connie, now retired in Florida.

She credits in particular Martha Giudici, who taught generations of Unity ministers, for explaining universal principles in a way people could grasp.

"She was a really good teacher with the fundamentals. My mind resonated with her mind, just the idea of making them not too difficult to understand—not too wordy, not too high-falutin'. Just make them so people who might not know anything at all about Unity or metaphysics would be able to say, 'Oh, that makes sense.' This was my stab at it."

Within the Unity movement, the Five Principles caught on and are now used in most churches. They are handed to visitors and new members as a short explanation of the Unity teachings. They are the basis of sermons, classes, debate and discussion. Connie is a little surprised at their longevity.

"There's certainly nothing new in them. I didn't invent anything. I just restated what the truth is, the way we teach it as I understand it."

I arrived at ministerial school several years after Connie's article was published, and I memorized the Five Principles as required. They didn't begin to grow on me until I was ministering in a church. I used them as a teaching tool, found myself referring to at least one of them in every Sunday lesson, and found myself using them in my daily life. They worked for me in the most ordinary situations and also addressed some of the great questions of humanity. Their truth reaches far beyond the Unity movement because principles, remember, are the same for everyone, all the time. I have come to believe Connie was divinely inspired the day she wrote these five statements of principles.

A great deal has been offered about spiritual principles in recent decades. Books and seminar leaders cite principles of prosperity, love, health, business and so on. For me, the Five Principles comprise them all. I believe they can be applied to any situation that shows up in our world. Other teachers might not agree, including some Unity ministers; we pride ourselves on offering a big tent for varying interpretations of the laws of life. Just as scientists, economists and historians look at facts differently, so do spiritual teachers. The beliefs surrounding the Five Principles that are expressed in this book are my own, and I fully expect e-mails and lively discussion with those who believe differently.

Indeed, many people have tinkered with Connie's original rendering of the Five Principles, so other versions exist with different wording. There is even a children's version (included in the back of this book). Don't be distracted by the specific language. Pay attention to the essence of the teachings. Work with these principles, test them, apply them to your life, and see what happens.

As well as offering tools for daily living, the Five Principles suggest answers to the great questions of existence that humans have been asking since the dawn of conscious awareness.

- What is this greater Presence that we sense around us?
- How can we communicate with this Presence?
- Who and what are we?
- Why do things happen in our lives the way they do?
- What are we on Earth to do?

Every religion and philosophical tradition offers answers to these fundamental questions. The myths that recur throughout history are attempts to answer them.

The Bible addresses them too. The story of Adam and Eve asks: Why is life so difficult? Why do we work so hard to grow food? Why is childbirth so painful? Early writers concluded that humans must have disobeyed God.

Their understanding sufficed for thousands of years: The circumstances of our survival seemed to be the result of pleasing or displeasing the Presence that permeated our lives. This Presence was conceptualized in many different ways and addressed accordingly. Maybe the sun god was angry. Maybe a virgin needed to be sacrificed. Maybe God required his human son to be crucified. Our ancestors did their best to answer the great questions of life.

As science has explained more and more about how the world works, we have become less superstitious but perhaps no less fearful. We still wonder why bad things happen to good people or rail against God as cold and uncaring. Many of us still aren't sure why we are on Earth or what kind of relationship is possible between us and the Presence.

We learn the secrets of life as we go, growing through our failures and successes. Those who have gone before have left us with many, many writings and signposts about what works and what doesn't. They discovered that two plus two is always four. They discovered that gravity holds us to the Earth. They discovered that spiritual laws are in effect for everyone, working all the time with no favorites and no changes.

The Five Principles offers a glimpse of what those laws are.

A Word About God

In my church, we began every Sunday service by saying that we honored "the many names for God and the many paths to God." I know a great many deeply spiritual people who firmly resist the word *God*. Please accept it in this book as shorthand for All That Is, the Ultimate Reality, the Presence that human beings have sensed within and around them for millennia.

I have used a variety of names and descriptions for the divine, but you may substitute whatever concepts or names work for you. I also invite you to release any baggage or stereotypes the word *God* carries for you and open yourself to new understanding.

Principle One

God is Absolute Good, everywhere present.

In Jesus' Words ...

The Father and I are one.
—John 10:30

Even though you do not believe me, believe the works,
that you may know and understand that
the Father is in me, and I in the Father.
—John 10:38

If you know me, you will know my Father also.
From now on, you do know him and have seen him.
—John 14:7

Chapter One

God Is All

If I had one wish for the world, it would be that every adult reexamine his or her view of God at least once per decade. God may not change, but people do, and we outgrow our old concepts. The ideas about God that we held at six will not serve us at sixteen and certainly not sixty. Just as children may outgrow peanut butter and opt for spicy curries, we can assimilate more and different ideas about the universe and its workings as we evolve.

Instead of changing their thinking, however, too many people simply throw away their belief in a higher power and, with it, the divine guidance, wisdom and comfort that could enrich their lives.

My childhood view of God was an old man in the sky, watching my every move. This God loved me, I was told, but this God refused to love anyone who didn't profess faith in Jesus and would send them to hell. And, by the way, God monitored my thoughts. I'd better be careful.

I simply didn't believe it, even in those early days of Sunday school. I'll always be grateful that the message of God's love was louder. I remember sitting in the church pew, so young that my feet didn't touch the floor, wondering what kind of God would condemn people to hell even if they had never heard of Jesus.

Yet at eight years old, I bravely walked alone to the front of my family's church in West Texas to profess my faith in Jesus, and on a Sunday night not long after, I was baptized. The silver-haired pastor put a handkerchief over my face and held my nose as he dunked me in the cool, chlorinated water of the baptistry. I did believe in the love of Jesus, but I also remember thinking, "I haven't done anything bad enough that Jesus had to die for my sins."

In college, I abandoned church and its teachings about God as I understood them. I couldn't pretend to believe anymore, especially having learned in my required religion courses that the Bible was written by human beings and that a number of books were left out. I was dismayed to hear that most of what we considered Christian teaching was devised hundreds of years after Jesus by councils of men with political agendas. I was astonished that the myth of a virgin mother whose divine son died and rose again was an ancient expression of the collective unconscious, long predating Christianity. Without the literal truth of the Bible stories, faith to me seemed a sham.

After college, I began to worship work instead. I spent 20 years without a spiritual rudder that might have guided me through early adulthood. By forty, I was professionally successful, financially secure and spiritually empty.

I know now that my story is fairly typical, except that the emptiness seems to be setting in sooner with each generation. Simple and concrete explanations about God wore out for me and, rather than investigate further, I gave up any semblance of a spiritual life. I wasn't aware of alternatives. I knew only the dogma of my childhood church—a set of rules that no one could meet except Jesus, who was considered divine and perfect—and given such an all-or-nothing option, I chose nothing. I had no concept of God for grownups.

God for Grownups

What would a God for grownups be?

First, one that meets us where we are and welcomes our questioning, growing, changing and doubting. The idea that God is made in humans' image is usually leveled as a criticism of religion, but what else could God be? Our human minds cannot conceive of All That Is, cannot encompass a universe of spiritual laws and dimensions that we only guess about. Our world religions are but feeble attempts to describe our varied experience of the unknown. God is understood as best we can, and we need a growing, malleable image of God that expands with each spiritual insight we glean.

Second, God for grownups has to be more than Santa Claus. The Ground of All Being surely is not making a list of who's naughty or nice and arranging eternal reward or punishment for each. This God is the creative force behind sweeping galaxies and infinitesimal life forms, of bewildering fractal patterns and perfect seasonal cycles, of mind-blowing beauty and pure potential, the oak tree in the acorn, the child in a microscopic twist of DNA. God for grownups is far outside the human pattern of thinking. Any limits to God are our own.

Third, most people want to believe that God is involved in their lives. Humans have always intuited a Presence they could not see, a silent source of guidance, wisdom and support—even love—and have sought throughout history to connect with this power. The Five Principles offer an entirely new way to understand such a higher power and our relationship to it.

Are we allowed to make up our own God? Of course! It's called theology—the study of the divine and its relationship to the world. What kind of God could not handle the questions of pipsqueak humans? Even an ordinary parent can withstand the rebellion and back talk of her children as they separate themselves from home and family and later return in new, adult relationships. When we approach God as adults, we are the prodigal son, finally aware of the divine love that always has been available to us. We don't have to be forgiven; we were never judged. What greater purpose do we have than an eternal quest to understand and commune with the Presence, regardless of our uncertainty?

The older I get, the more I believe that finding some kind of spiritual understanding is a quality-of-life issue. Charles Fillmore, whose great-granddaughter Connie formulated the Five Principles, said in a 1924 sermon,

"You are alive, and you won't live very long unless you make contact with this spiritual side of your nature. People who think they live a span of life and call that living are not living at all. There is a great, substantial, eternal life right here present … and the object of our existence is to make contact with that life."[1] Fillmore lived to almost ninety-four, relishing every day.

Descriptions of the divine force in the world have blossomed into a fascinating array of expressions through the world's religions, and they have changed over time. The Bible itself is the story of humans' developing concepts of God described in a range of ways, from a harsh judge to a mother comforting her child. Jesus introduced a personal, paternal God that he called *Abba*, the Aramaic word for "papa" or "daddy."

The Bible also reflects the expanding consciousness of human beings, which continues today. Our task is to nurture the evolution of our own species, which will naturally include a deeper understanding of how the universe operates and our role in it. Quantum science now accompanies us on the journey.

Yet we struggle with words adequate to reflect our experience of the divine, and we haven't even begun to realign religious language with the discoveries of science. We will never understand the totality of the divine, but it permeates our lives nonetheless.

"Let us remember that by describing God with words in our human way, we are but stating in the lisping syllables of the child that which in its maturity the mind still only faintly grasps," Fillmore wrote. "Yet man may know God and become the vehicle and expression of God, the unlimited fount of life, health, light and love."[2]

Principle One allows me to know God in new ways and to stretch my understanding of All That Is: *God is Absolute Good, everywhere present.*

This principle seemed obvious to our animistic forebears, who perceived the action of Spirit in all forms of life. More recently, science and spirituality have begun to repair their false incompatibility and have made us more aware of the literal oneness of all things.

Principle One affirms that God is all there is. God is omnipotent, omniscient and omnipresent—not all-powerful but all power, not all-knowing but all knowledge, and present everywhere. God is the stars, the rocks, the animals, the people. God is the love, the creativity, the wisdom that human beings express. All that we are and have is God, and we can never be separate from that universal power.

We have lived so long with our childhood idea of God as an old man in the sky, keeping books on our behavior or at the very least watching from a distance, that we may struggle to bend our minds around the idea of our oneness with Being. Author John Shelby Spong, the retired Episcopal bishop who manages to demythologize Christianity while still believing in it, describes *theism* as a concept of God "external to our life, supernatural in power." This idea of worshipping an external God has become so ingrained in Christianity that anyone who believes differently is considered an *a-theist*.

As Christianity developed, theism not only became entrenched as church dogma but became our cultural understanding of God, at least in the West. People who have never been to a church can still describe this judging, intervening God. They either believe in it or they don't, but theism allows no alternatives. And theism is reinforced every time we refer to God as He or even She or describe a "God *who* …"

Spong elaborates: The theistic God is seen as "a being, supernatural in power, dwelling outside this world and able to invade the world in miraculous ways to bless, to punish, to accomplish divine will, to answer prayers, and to come to the aid of frail, powerless human beings."[3]

The Five Principles challenge every aspect of theism—what God is, what human beings are, how the two relate, how prayer works, and how we are expected to live as human beings.

The History of Oneness

Principle One maintains we are one with God—not separate, not being watched, but immersed in the divine. As the apostle Paul told the Athenians, we live and move and have our being in God.[4] And in oneness, God lives and moves and has expression in us.

A God of oneness is immanent and transcendent; that is, within us and all around us. We are like fish in water, largely unaware of the sustaining force in which we exist.

Putting oneness into words is not easy—believe me, it has been the greatest challenge of writing this book! Our minds are schooled in duality—hot and cold, up and down, good and bad, us and them. Most people have never questioned theism, in which God and humans are separate entities. Even the term "relationship with God" connotes duality, the connection of two beings.

Of course, our generations are not the first to face this linguistic challenge. Throughout history, humans have used myth and metaphor to try to illustrate the oneness that can only be experienced.

The writer of the Book of John resorted to lyrical, mystical language. "I am the vine; you are the branches. If a man remains in me and I in him, he will bear much fruit; apart from me you can do nothing."[5]

Again and again, Jesus spoke of his oneness with the Father, the divine. But this was not news. For thousands of years, humans had understood and tried to describe the unity of the universe.

The Buddhist sutras envisioned a net stretching in all directions. The Hopis spoke of Spider Grandmother, who spun a great web connecting all things. To the ancient Chinese, it was the Tao or flow of the universe. The Hymn of Creation from the Hindu Rig Veda speaks of the Absolute, called *Brahman*, and describes it as ultimate, eternal and beyond human description. This is the Ground of Being or Infinite Reality. We hear the names God, Holy Spirit, the Universe, the Way, Father-Mother, Creator, Divine, One Mind, Source Energy, First Cause and, thanks to Star Wars, the Force. It has also been named Allah, Buddha,

Christ, Kali, Shiva, Krishna and Kuan Yin, all concepts of the divine.

Physicist Max Planck, the originator of quantum theory, spoke of "conscious and intelligent mind." Astronaut Edgar Mitchell called it "Nature's Mind." In scientific terms, it is a field of pure potential, an energy that underlies all creation.

It is All That Is.

By me is this entire universe pervaded.
All things are in Me, and I in them.
Know that as the mighty wind blowing everywhere
rests in the sky,
all created beings rest in Me.
I am the Father, the Mother, the Supporter
and the Grandsire of the universe.
—Bhagavad Gita, 9:4,6,17

Humans have always sensed, have deeply understood, that there is an invisible foundation to the universe, a cohesiveness to all that we see and all that we are. We read it in sacred writings through the ages. We see it celebrated in rituals, burials, dance, song and art throughout time and cultures.

As All That Is, the energy that we call God cannot have any boundaries. An eternal life force cannot be an entity or supreme being with opinions or judgments. God simply is, the Source of all energy. Like the air that surrounds us, this Source, this Spirit, is available for our sustenance. We may take deep gulps of air or hold our breath until we turn blue. Air, both within us and all around us, is not watching or judging our behavior. It does not insert itself into our experience. On the day we stop breathing, air does not notice.

"God is principle. By principle is meant definite, exact and unchangeable rules of action," wrote Fillmore.

"From the teaching that the Deity is a person, we have come to believe that God is changeable; that He gets angry with His people and condemns them; that some are chosen or favored above others; that in His sight good and evil are verities, and that He defends the one and deplores the other. We must relieve our minds of these ideas of a personal God ruling over us in an arbitrary, manlike manner." [6]

The idea that God is spiritual law is an impersonal concept, and we're not going to stop there. But it's helpful to know that humans live according to a set of principles that operate for our use and survival. The Five Principles sum up how they work.

Yes, But What About Evil?

The principle of oneness—that we are in God and God is in us, that we are one with each other and with all the universe—may be lovely and inspiring on the surface, but it is difficult to describe and even more difficult to live. Furthermore, in my experience, people are often shocked by the ramifications of a world where everything, absolutely everything, is the divine.

The most common question is this: If God is good and God is all there is, how can evil exist in the world?

Such questions are a recurring theme when studying the Five Principles. If humans are divine expressions of God (Principle Two), how can they behave so badly? If we are the creators of our own experience (Principle Three), why would we ever create unpleasantness?

No single answer suffices. Indeed, humans have been trying to understand why bad things happen to good people since they first became conscious of themselves. The Christian answer—that humans are born sinful—contradicts Principle Two, which states we are divine expressions of God and inherently good. We are not born in original sin but original blessing, created in God's image and likeness. And yet anyone who turns on the news will witness man's inhumanity to man and might understandably question any teaching that claims Absolute Good in the universe.

The Absolute is not where we live as humans; it is the plane of the divine, a realm where everything exists as a perfect idea. The physical or earthly form of those ideas is rarely perfect. Human beings, for instance, are the physical expression of the perfect idea of male and female, yet we know that our bodies and behavior are not perfect in the manifest realm—that is, on the relative plane of existence where ideas become physical reality. We live on this dense, three-dimensional human plane with all its drama and emotion. But as spiritual beings having a human experience, we are never disconnected from Absolute perfection.

Through the years, I have put together a list of possible explanations for the events we consider evil.

It's cosmic effrontery, I know. The question of evil's existence has been asked for millennia, has been wrestled with by theologians, students, clergy and ordinary people who are suffering, and humans still don't have a definitive answer. But this list sorts out some possibilities. Consider:

- Humans were created with free will, and we make mistakes. The word *sin* originally meant missing the mark. Some miss it by miles.

- Good and evil are simply labels that humans give to events, based on our opinions at the time. What first appears to be a tragedy may turn out to be a blessing.

- The human species is immature. The Aramaic word that became *evil* in the Bible is *bisha*, which means "immature" or "unripe." Hence the biblical reference to "evil fruit." It wasn't ripe. We as humans are immature or unripe, not yet living from divine consciousness.

- We can't see the big picture. Events have meaning we do not understand, although later we might see the gifts that were brought to us through the most difficult times in our lives.

- We are creating our world through consciousness (Principle Three), which most people do not realize much less know how to handle. Our every thought, feeling and word sets up a response from the universe, but we have only a glimmer of understanding how to create our experience deliberately.

- What we call evil is an expression of mass consciousness. We all contribute to it through our angry and violent thoughts, the energetic vibrations we pour into the One Mind. The energy inevitably expresses somewhere, just as an erupting volcano releases heat from the Earth.
- We are balancing the events of a past life, sometimes called *karma*. This is not so much punishment or reward as reconciling accounts and offering an opportunity to experience life from all sides.

These theories reflect the imperfection of human beings but not the existence of a force of evil. If God is All That Is, then there can be no other power. No devil, no Satan, no Adversary doing battle for our souls or luring us to the dark side. If God is Absolute Good, then what we consider evil cannot be real or permanent. Understand, it can be painful, but it stems from humans' misuse of spiritual law, not from an evil entity that overtakes us. War, terrorism, crime, starvation, ignorance and destructive competition for resources are human constructs, based on fear, arrogance and greed.

"The belief in a supernatural source of evil is not necessary. Men alone are quite capable of every wickedness,"[7] wrote Joseph Conrad, the English writer who explored the tension between good and evil within each of us.

Although people who believe that evil has no reality are often accused of irresponsible optimism, the evidence shows that evil eventually breaks down. It has no permanence. In my lifetime alone, I have seen the end of oppressive dictatorships in Eastern Europe and apartheid in South Africa, and the progress of the civil rights movement in the United States. Persecution and violence are condemned; human rights are championed.

Good eventually wins out. The Wicked Witch melts, Darth Vader is revealed as a damaged pretender, Voldemort is destroyed by his own malevolence. These are fictional characters, yes, but they reflect our collective journey. Deep down, we know how the story always ends.

As we grapple with questions of evil and suffering, we could just as easily ask: Why is there good? Why do so many things turn out well? How is it that clouds have silver linings and blessings come in disguise? If what we call God is a creative life energy that is not intervening to bless us, then what are we doing right? And how do we define "good" anyway, except that everything goes our way?

Indeed, we are not perfect. Our evolution is toward a consciousness of oneness, toward good, but we have far yet to go.

Yes, But Terrible Things Happen

My midlife search for spirituality led me to Unity, which is part of the New Thought theological movement that developed in the United States in the late 1800s. I eventually became a minister and realized over the years that I was using at least one of the Five Principles in every sermon. They seemed to work in any situation.

But nothing upset my congregation more than my suggesting evil is not real, that it has no power of itself; it has only the power we give it. After one such sermon, one of my favorite elderly women came through the receiving line, reached up to pat my cheek, and said cheerfully, "I disagreed with everything you said!"

Most people bestow tremendous power onto those human beings we consider evil, who cause or threaten harm to others, even though we know they are acting from their own pain or fear.

Would ignoring evil disarm it? Don't dismiss the idea. As we have declared a War on Terror, a War on Drugs, a War on Poverty, a War on Crime, the problems only seem to have grown bigger. We cling to the notion of evil as a detrimental, unpredictable force in our world and refuse any suggestion that it is not real. We argue for our fears about terrorism or climate change or economic instability, heatedly trying to prove that things are only getting worse. And in doing so, we reinforce the principle that what we focus on grows. We create our experience by where we place our attention. What we resist, persists.

A simple example: Imagine the local news reports that a burglar has been breaking into homes in your neighborhood. Those who see the report buy extra locks, put bars on the windows, and sleep with a gun nearby. Those who don't see the report go about their business, oblivious and happy.

The spiritual goal is to acknowledge there might be a burglar *and* to live without fear, to hold a consciousness of well-being. Most people wrap their fears around them like a coat of armor, somehow assuming that fear and worry protect them from What Might Happen. As we shall see with Principle Three, fear is a magnet that draws to us exactly what we don't want. "What I feared has come upon me; what I dreaded has happened to me," Job said, uttering a spiritual truth that we still have not comprehended.[8]

To grant evil a power of its own would be to accept it as inevitable. I much prefer to think of evil as a result of human error. Then we can do something about it! The Holocaust, Rwanda, Darfur and every other example of human immaturity run amok don't have to happen again. We can indeed change the world by changing our thinking, by evolving consciously as a species.

The alternative is to believe we are at the mercy of forces opposing us—good battling evil, God vs. The Enemy, you against others, victory or defeat. A great many people hold that view. When anything goes wrong, they reassure themselves that they are victims of a dangerous world. Taking responsibility for ourselves as cocreators with God is far less popular and a lot more work.

The disadvantage to empowering the idea of evil is that life becomes one long battle, an uphill trek, a long overcoming. No sooner do we win out over one challenge than we attract another. We create our own misery through our belief in adversity and the power we give it to destroy us. It is as if we let ourselves be trapped in a dark room, agitated and fearful, yet never reaching for the light switch.

Imagine living instead in our oneness with God. Life would still have its human difficulties, but our view of them would be changed. Rather than battling an outer enemy, we would take charge of our lives from within. We would transcend our labels of what is good or bad and live in the flow of the universe. Nothing might change in our outer circumstances, but our interpretation of them, our understanding, would take on new meaning.

Life is consciousness. What we hold in mind shows up as our reality. *Mind*, in this usage, comprises thoughts, feelings and beliefs centered in the brain and heart. If you want to know what's in your consciousness, look around at your life. The universe has delivered whatever you focused on, expected and believed, consciously or not. With your own divine power, you are the creator of your experience. (We will explore the mechanics of this in Principle Three.)

In the Absolute Realm, all is One. God is all there is. God is Absolute Good. We might never comprehend the Ground of Being while we are in human form. But we know it and sense it, and we can learn to trust it.

"It does not matter how many poor people you see, or how many crippled or sick or unhappy people there are in the world; that does not alter the fact that the One Principle is good and, when used intelligently, will destroy every manner of lack, limitation or disease exactly as light destroys darkness," wrote Venice Bloodworth in *Key to Yourself*, a profound little book about the laws by which we live.[9]

God does not ride to the rescue. What we call God is a force of energy, not a supernatural being that intervenes in our lives. How that divine energy expresses, or doesn't, is up to us. But as we will learn with Principles Two and Three, we have far more power to order our world than we realize. We are one with All That Is.

***

"I want to beg you, dear friend, as well as I can, to have patience with everything that remains unsolved in your heart. Try to love the questions themselves ..."
—Rainer Maria Rilke, *Letters to a Young Poet*[10]

Meditation

on Principle One

I enter into the stillness to align myself with the One Mind, the One Presence that permeates all of creation. I feel myself as a part of this creation, connected to all of nature. I am the light and darkness, I am the oceans and the land. I am the rocks and trees, the fish and birds, the beasts of the Earth, and I am one with every human being on the planet. In this oneness, I sense the order of all things. I feel the divine love that moves in me and in every molecule of the cosmos. I know the divine intelligence that is the foundation of all that is or ever will be. I am one with All.

Principle Two

Human beings have a spark of divinity within them,
the Christ spirit within. Their very essence is of God,
and therefore they are also inherently good.

In Jesus' Words ...

Jesus answered them,
"Is it not written in your Law,
'I have said you are gods'?"
—John 10:34

Very truly I tell you, the one who believes in me
will also do the works that I do
and, in fact, will do greater works than these ...
—John 14:12

As you go, preach this message:
"The kingdom of heaven is near."
—Matthew 10:7

Chapter Two

You Are God

What is the point of spiritual growth? Seriously, if God is not a wrathful deity keeping tabs on our behavior and poised to send us to hell, why is it important to follow a spiritual path? To be a good and moral person? To feel happier or make people like us?

With Principle One, we broaden our understanding of God to a field of love and intelligence that is the foundation of the universe. God is not a supreme being watching, judging, parenting or protecting us, but rather the substance of all that exists, including us. In that light, we need to reevaluate who we are as human beings and revisit the roles we are called to play in creation.

Most people still want to believe in a God that knows and cares about the details of their lives, that can make a difference in what happens or at least in how they feel about what happens. Even with a concept of God as the Ground of Being, as impervious to our dramas as the air we breathe, that personal relationship with the divine has not been lost. With Principle Two, it merely has been relocated—inside you, *as you.*

Every culture and religion has a creation story, an explanation of how the Earth and its inhabitants came to be. Some cite creation *ex nihilo*, created from nothing. Some believe humans were literally molded from dust and ashes and will return to the Earth after death. More recently, we have come to know ourselves as stardust; the atoms of our bodies are the remains of supernovas that exploded and cast their elements into the galaxy. But wherever we originated physically, we were first an idea in God-Mind. And if God is all there is and everything is God, how could we be anything but divine? *Imago Dei*—the image of God.

When I was still new to this spiritual path, I was assured by books and teachers that all the answers and guidance I needed were within me. I was alarmed! I knew the confusion that lurked within; that's why I was seeking spiritual guidance in middle age. I knew that living according to my ideas and my will hadn't been enough for me. If God was within me, then I would be praying to myself, and that was a hopeless proposition!

It took years for me to understand a new concept of Self in which I am an expression of God. It helped when I formed a new concept of God that is both transcendent (all there is, everywhere) and immanent (personal, within).

The best example I know to describe our divinity compares humans to God like waves on the ocean. Each of us is distinct as a wave yet made up of precisely the energy and attributes of Mother Ocean itself. We are not the whole ocean, but we are the same composition, nothing more or less, part of the divine flow.[1]

People who insist that humans are divine are often accused of thinking they are God, and the secret is: We are! Just as every tree is God in expression, just as every sunset or newborn child or act of mercy allows us to witness the divine, we, too, are expressions of God on Earth. We are the divine expressing in human form. At first it may sound grandiose to claim it, but properly understood, the awareness of our own divinity is where we derive our comfort, guidance and strength for the human experience. We can never be separate from God, and we have only begun to tap the power of the human spirit.

This is what Jesus tried so many times to tell us and show us. Jesus was demonstrating what is possible for human beings when we are fully aligned with the presence of God within us. He was able to love and forgive, heal and teach because he was living from his God Self or the Christ Presence within him, and he said we could do the same. His single life changed the course of human history. The same divine essence Jesus had dwells in each of us, imperfect as we are.

This is the crux of Principle Two, that we are expressions of the divine in human form, that our essence is God.

Of course, considering ourselves to be on a par with Jesus—even in potential—is shocking to some. But imagine Jesus as a wave in the ocean, saying to the others, "See, we are all made of the same water, salt and minerals. We are all expressing the power of nature."

He might have been a larger wave—like the enormous, curling surf in Hawaii—but his intention was never to be revered as anything other than what we are. Indeed, his primary message was inclusivity.

The belief that Jesus demonstrated the potential for all was widely understood in the years between Jesus' earthly ministry and the development of the early church. With practical and political pressures intruding from all sides, the church became sharply divided about who Jesus was and what his life meant. His teaching that *"You* are the light of the world"[2] competed with the idea that Jesus—and only Jesus—was divine. The interpretation of Jesus' life as evidence of our human potential was officially rejected when the first uniform Christian doctrine was decreed by the Council of Nicaea in 325. But Christian mystics throughout the ages have continued to experience the intimate oneness with the divine that Jesus had and that he called us to discover within ourselves.

Jesus was not asking to be worshipped; he was showing us who we are and what we can do. He repeatedly expressed frustration that his disciples didn't get it. When his disciples could not cure an epileptic boy, Jesus exclaimed in exasperation: "You faithless and perverse generation, how much longer must I be with you? How much longer must I put up with you?"[3] His final words of forgiveness—"They do not know what they are doing"[4]—might have been a lament for us all.

Although we can never be certain of any of Jesus' actual words, the experience of Jesus—as the story was remembered and retold, passed down, and finally written down decades later—was that he embodied the divine. People who knew Jesus felt they had encountered God. As we discover our own Christ nature, we "come to the Father" or become more aware of the divine energy that animates each of us.

No less an authority than comedian Bill Cosby told a Detroit audience in 2007, "People are waiting around for Jesus to come, when Jesus is already within you."[5]

Indeed, this is what Jesus meant by "I am the way, the truth and the life. No one comes to the Father except through me."[6] He was speaking as the Christ, the divine that dwells within us all. It is through the Spirit within that we know our oneness with God. No intercession is necessary, any more than the ocean wave needs to be reconciled with the ocean.

Our job as humans is to revive this spiritual truth in the world and to live from the Christ of our being, the part of us that is God, our divine core.

What If God Were One of Us?

Over the years, I have come to a visceral understanding that Spirit is who I truly am, as the image and likeness of God, and that I have all the attributes of God latent within me. Knowing I can rely on this divine Self is not an exaggerated sense of my own powers; it is just the opposite. It is humbly turning to the divine within for insight and wisdom. It is discovering God to be closer than breathing, nearer than hands and feet.[7]

The point of spiritual growth, then, is to know myself as Spirit and express it in my life.

Growing up, many of us were taught that following a spiritual path required behaving well lest God be disappointed. As adults some of us still try to be spiritual by walking a straight and narrow path through sheer willpower. It means doing the honest thing, being nice when we don't feel like it, resisting the various temptations of the flesh. Or not, sometimes. And through it all, our egos are busy comparing us to everyone else and assuring us that we either come out on top or on bottom, smugly superior or dismally lacking.

What if it were possible to rise above such human travails and live effortlessly with an attitude of love and compassion for yourself and others? What if you could hold onto thoughts and feelings so positive that only good would be drawn into your life? What if you could clear out the debris of the past and any fears about the future so thoroughly that Spirit could shine from within you and light up the world?

That is the point of spiritual growth. It is living from the Christ within, making decisions from the higher Self, loving with the unconditional and inexhaustible energy of the divine, contributing to the well-being of the planet. It is to express effortlessly who we truly are.

Every human being knows this Self already, at least to some extent. It is the inner witness that watches your life unfold and is conscious of your existence. It is the intuitive nudge that prompts you to take an un-expected turn in life—even if you ignore it—and that propels you to be more and better. It is a still small voice that is sometimes as difficult to distinguish as a whisper at a rock concert, more sensed than heard, and yet persistent.

This divine Presence that dwells within you meets your busy, everyday human self in the soul. The soul is part of the Eternal You that has come to Earth for a human experience, built a physical body, and begun to operate on this planet through the ego. The ego is the functioning human, the part of us that gets up and gets through the day using a brain and five senses. The ego is not a bad thing; it just forgets that it is not alone, not carrying the entire burden of our survival. It tends to overreact.

Picture the four essential parts of every human like Russian nesting dolls. The smallest is the body, which is essentially a spacesuit that allows us to survive in the Earth environment. Then the ego, which, in its healthy state, gives us the focus and confidence to function in the human world. The soul is an eternal, individualized creation that grows, learns and seeks ever-closer union with God. And Spirit—present in everything, everyone, everywhere—is God, the One, the same for all of us and always available as the essence of who we are.

Notice: You do not *have* a soul. You *are* a soul that has a body and an ego, or personality. I believe that our souls come to Earth to learn and grow, and they glean more from each lifetime. Imagine how much faster we could evolve with conscious spiritual growth! That would mean putting the soul in charge of our lives rather than the ego. That is the evolutionary drive we feel for the human species—not to adapt our bodies to Earth environment, like animals and plants, but to adapt our egos so that we express from the soul. We will never be egoless—we need our egos to function—but we can put the ego in service to the soul.

This means giving up our attachment to the dramas of the human experience, the stories we tell ourselves about being victims and heroes, celebrities and nobodies, in danger or in triumph, in love or in loss. Pretty much any event that could make up the lyrics of a country song is an expression of ego.

Living from the soul doesn't mean we will avoid all difficulties, but we will see and handle them differently. Asking "what would Jesus do?" may not be useful in figuring out how to force ourselves to be better behaved. But it might be a clue to what our lives would look like if we were living in soul consciousness, integrating the human and spiritual beings that we are.

Fortunately, the process of moving from ego to soul is a popular spiritual topic and is being addressed everywhere. The whole culture of alternative healing, meditation, spiritual reading and study, progressive churches, spiritual counseling and even some cutting-edge business practices is designed to nurture the soul and bring forth Spirit in each of us.

Yes, But Humans Don't Act Divine

If we consider that we are made in God's image and are expressions of the divine, we surely are led to ask: Why do people behave so badly?

First, we can give ourselves a break through neuroscience. Our human brains simply haven't caught up with modern life. Large parts of the brain still operate in the primitive realm, seeking only food, sex and safety. We are no longer in danger from lions and tigers, but our bodies are flooded with the fight-or-flight responses triggered by the stress of everyday life, even though it is rarely life-threatening. Most of our egos' excesses are misguided attempts to protect us.

It's not easy to override these ancient drives with the prefrontal cortex, the logical, analytical brain behind our high human foreheads. This newest part of the brain considers alternatives and understands consequences—in other words, it gives us the maturity that forestalls "evil"—the *bisha* Jesus spoke about. This is the seat of self-awareness. This is where we envision our futures and become motivated to act in our own best interests.[8]

The prefrontal lobe is at work when we think through a decision. It is also where mystics have located the third eye of intuition. But sometimes animal instincts overtake us before either human logic or spiritual intuition has a chance. Thus we have yet another theory of why evil exists in the world. Jesus and others showed us what it looks like when we live from the higher Self and call forth the compassion and cooperation that exist in us naturally. But we still grapple with the physiological imperatives of a bygone era.

Think of it this way: If the 14-billion-year history of the universe were compressed into a century, Earth would have existed for just the last 33 years and *homo sapiens* for only the past day.[9] No wonder we live imperfectly as humans! We are still at the beginning of our evolution.

How do we override our primitive instincts? Jesus taught us to focus on consciousness rather than behavior. The Jewish laws prescribed certain behaviors in every facet of life, and the Pharisees continually questioned Jesus about the letter of the law. Time and again, he referred to their scriptures—"You've heard it said"—then gave a new teaching—"but I tell you." When Jesus said anger was as bad as murder, or lust equaled adultery, he was talking about its effect in consciousness, the combination of thoughts, beliefs and feelings that make us who we are.

And who are we, as human beings?

One of the bleakest answers I have run across was a statement of faith from Marketplace Chaplains, a national evangelical group that provides chaplains to corporations. This group performs great works of compassion yet believes human beings are "born into the world with a nature which not only possesses no spark of divine life, but is essentially and unchangeably unholy apart from divine grace." Because of original sin, it said, this "total depravity of human nature has been transmitted to the entire human race of man, the Man Christ Jesus alone being excepted."[10]

If everything is God (Principle One), then there can be no part of ourselves that is not divine (Principle Two). There is no war raging between the human and spiritual sides of us. That sounds too much like Satan trying to woo our souls, although in many circles "ego" has replaced the devil as our nemesis. Beware of any theory that paints human/ego as bad and soul/Spirit as good. That is duality in a universe where, in fact, all is One. We came to Earth as spiritual beings to have a human experience, and all of it is valuable.

The good news, in terms of behavior, is that we are wired for morality. Laws and commandments are merely the written descriptions of behavior that each civilization has realized will promote well-being for the whole.

Eckhart Tolle in *A New Earth* ruminated on the steadying influence of the Christ within:

> Jesus speaks of the innermost I Am, the essence identity of every man and woman, every life-form, in fact. He speaks of the life that you are. Some Christian mystics have called it the Christ within; Buddhists call it your Buddha nature; for Hindus, it is Atman, the indwelling God. When you are in touch with that dimension within yourself—and being in touch with it is your natural state, not some

miraculous achievement—all your actions and relationships will reflect the oneness with all life that you sense deep within. This is love. Law, commandments, rules and regulations are necessary for those who are cut off from who they are, the Truth within. They prevent the worst excesses of the ego, and often they don't even do that. "Love and do what you will," said St. Augustine. Words cannot get much closer to the Truth than that.[11]

Or as the apostle Paul put it, "Christ in you, the hope of glory."[12]

Yes, But What About Hitler and Osama Bin Laden?

Another popular theory about why humans experience both bliss and trauma at each other's hands is that we come into human form with soul contracts. I like to imagine our souls together in groups on the Other Side, planning their lives on Earth. Each soul has a purpose for acquiring a body and living as a human for a while. Various souls offer to play various roles, like a screenplay or like children playing house. "I'll be the mommy and you be the daddy this time." A soul contract.

Exactly what happens once they're on Earth is not predetermined, but most times the souls will find each other and carry out the roles they volunteered to play.

This idea is delightfully explored in a children's book, *The Little Soul and the Sun*, by Neale Donald Walsch, who wrote the *Conversations With God* series.

In his story, a little soul is planning a human lifetime to work on forgiveness.

Another soul offers to accompany him to Earth. "I will help you," she says. "I can come into your next lifetime and do something for you to forgive!"[13]

So *that's* why the most difficult people in our lives are sometimes considered our greatest teachers! Maybe we planned it. Maybe at a soul level, we asked for our lessons, especially the ones that force our growth.

Maybe Hitler and Osama Bin Laden played their roles to push the world toward greater peace, to make us aware of our oneness and our desire to evolve past violence. Some people might make choices that others label bad or even evil, but who is to say they are not playing their parts perfectly for the overall growth of our species?

Does being divine mean being perfect? Perhaps we can be divine—growing, changing, evolving expressions of God—and still make mistakes, like a toddler who falls down while learning to walk. Perhaps we contain the potential for expressing perfectly, just as an acorn contains the potential for a perfect oak tree but has to grow and develop to allow that perfection to express. What constitutes the perfect human, anyway? What is the perfect sunset? The perfect flower? Each of us has different personalities, different skills and talents, different interests that make us who we are.

One thing we know from the study of biology is that crisis drives evolution. Plants and animals change in response to stress in their environment. Some manage to adapt, some don't. One key to survival is learning to cooperate with other species.

Consider an old-growth forest, with trees, plants and animals each supporting the other, the high leaves shading delicate flowers on the ground, then dying and dropping to nourish the Earth for more growth. Insects pollinate flowers. Birds drop fertilizer and seeds. Natural cooperation.

This is what the human species has yet to learn, says biologist Elisabet Sahtouris in her book *EarthDance*: "We see ourselves in the context of our planet's biological evolution as a still new, experimental species with developmental stages that parallel the stages of our individual development. From this perspective, humanity is now in adolescent crisis and, just because of that, stands on the brink of maturity in a position to achieve true humanity in the full meaning of that word."[14]

Humans, even as violent as we seem to be, are the first species to understand that we have the capacity to change. This means we can evolve consciously, the most exciting development so far in our brief human history. We can choose who we want to be as individuals and explore ways to cooperate as groups. We are responsible not only for our own evolution but how evolution continues to unfold on the planet. If we learn to cooperate as a mature species, we still won't all desire or believe the same things—any more than a tree, a bird and a deer become alike—but we will align our self-interests with the well-being of all others and the Earth. In other words, we will create the kingdom of heaven together.

This, too, is the point of pursuing spiritual growth, not only to evolve ourselves but our world. Jesus assured us that the kingdom of heaven was at hand, among us, already here. Heaven and hell are states of consciousness that we create for ourselves while in human form. And as expressions of the divine, heaven is our natural habitat.

"The kingdom is inside of you, and it is outside of you," Jesus is quoted in the Gospel of Thomas, a book of Jesus' sayings that was left out of the Bible.

"When you come to know yourselves, then you will become known, and you will realize that it is you who are the sons of the living Father. But if you will not know yourselves, you dwell in poverty and it is you who are that poverty."[15]

We are equipped for building the kingdom, one choice at a time, through our conscious contact with Supreme Wholeness. We are never separate from God because we are God. We have grown out of creation like the trees and flowers. Identifying the process as evolution makes it no less divine, no less a miracle. Even as science continues to investigate how we came into being, our spiritual work is to answer *why*.

Yes, But What About Salvation?

Are we sinners who need to be saved? Yes and no. We surely are not perfect. We make mistakes, we miss the mark. Indeed we cause incalculable suffering for each other. But there is no angry god who will send us to hell unless we believe certain religious doctrine. The Earth has received many teachers who assured us of our oneness with each other and the universe. Forgiveness is a given; we are never judged by the force of love that underlies all things. We live in a state of grace. The universe is biased in our favor.

We are redeemed not because we behave well or adopt specific religious beliefs but because that's how the world works. From each crisis comes growth and renewal, biologically and spiritually. Redemption means to repair for the better, to restore. It is the alchemy of turning metal to gold, bad to good, lemons to lemonade. For Christians, it is the story of Easter, rising from the dead to live again.

The Easter metaphor of crucifixion, tomb and resurrection reflects our lives as they play out over and over. The worst of our experiences can become the greatest blessings of our lives. The darkest human behavior can move us to compassion and to the expression of our higher selves. Remember the global outpouring of love and our sense of oneness on September 11, 2001? With our response to a terrorist attack, we glimpsed who we truly are and what the kingdom of heaven can be. Love outweighs violence, our human oneness trumps our differences. As we continue to call on the best of ourselves—whether we call it the prefrontal cortex or the divine within—we consciously evolve for the better.

We carry out this task day to day by mastering Principle Three.

***

"I want to offer the possibility that Jesus was, as he proclaimed, a savior. Not the savior, not the one and only Son of God. Rather, Jesus embodied the highest level of enlightenment. He spent his brief adult life describing it, teaching it and passing it on to future generations. Jesus intended to save the world by showing others the path to God-consciousness."

—Deepak Chopra, *The Third Jesus*[16]

Meditation

on Principle Two

As I turn within, I retreat from outer awareness and enter my Soul, the divine in me. It is here that I know my connection to Spirit. Deep within, I find the peace that passes understanding. Deep within, I find the knowledge of all things and the awareness of absolute good. Deep within, I touch the gifts that are God. It is here that I receive wisdom and guidance, that I know truth and understanding, that I am strengthened and comforted. This is the divine essence that I am. The core of me is God. And from the God within me, I can do anything.

Principle Three

Human beings create their experiences
by the activity of their thinking. Everything in
the manifest realm has its beginning in thought.

In Jesus' Words …

The measure you give
will be the measure you get back.
—Luke 6:38

I will give you the keys of the kingdom of heaven, and
whatever you bind on earth will be bound in heaven,
and whatever you loose on earth will be loosed in
heaven.
—Matthew 16:19

Do not be afraid, little flock, it is your Father's
good pleasure to give you the kingdom.
—Luke 12:32

Ask and it will be given to you; search and you will
find; knock and the door will be opened for you.
—Matthew 7:7

Chapter Three

Cocreating With God

Now the fun begins!

As we come to believe, to truly understand the first two principles, we begin to see that we are living in an ocean of love and abundance in which we cannot fail. We are ever connected to the Source of all things. We are extensions of the Ultimate Creator. And we can tap into the power, wisdom and guidance of the divine at any time.

What amazing power we have as human beings! No less than the abilities of the Christ reside in us. And what awesome responsibility! If we truly can do all the works that Jesus did "and more than these," as stated in John 14:12, we can change our lives and our world. We are cocreators with God.

Cocreation is another spiritual idea that struck me as blasphemous when I first heard it. I still believed God was an autocratic ruler and I was a worm of the dust. How could I possibly create?

We are made in the image and likeness of God, and God is, if anything, a Creator, the intelligence behind all that we know. If we are expressions of a Creator, how could we be anything but creative? Not just creative in the sense of art and inventions but creators of life as we know it.

This is Principle Three. Our thoughts, feelings and beliefs have the power to create our reality. And while I think of it as cocreating with God, the law also works for those with no concept of God. Like any universal law, it is in effect for everyone, the same way, all the time.

This idea of our innate creative power has become more widespread recently, although it is ancient wisdom. The Buddha said 2500 years ago, "All that we are is the result of what we have thought. If a man speaks or acts with an evil thought, pain follows him … If a man speaks or acts with a pure thought, happiness follows him, like a shadow that never leaves him."[1]

The creative power of our thoughts has been variously called the Law of Attraction, the Law of Mind Action, the Science of Mind, the Art of Allowing and the Secret. It has been ridiculed, dismissed, mislabeled, misunderstood and misapplied, yet it works. It is a spiritual principle that governs our lives, whether we know it or not, whether we believe it or not. We are creating with every thought and feeling.

Once again, quantum science helps us understand a law of life that until now was simply intuited and practiced by spiritual masters. Not only is there no predestination for our lives, no blueprint or fate, but we are choosing moment to moment what happens to us and for us. In fact, God's ongoing creation happens *through* us, through our consciousness, our collection of thoughts, feelings and beliefs.

We choose with our *focus*. We face a universe of unlimited possibilities, and we choose which one becomes "real" for us by focusing on that possibility. Every possible outcome already exists in potential, but we draw forth our reality with our expectations and anticipation. *Whether we want it or not.* If we are focused on a particular outcome, it shows up.

This is why metaphysicians emphasize positive thinking. Not because the cheerful are rewarded by a supreme being. Not because magical thinking comes true. But because we live in a universe where our thoughts—conscious or unconscious—bring about the events of our lives.

Scary, isn't it? And magnificent.

It means if we don't like our lives, we can change them. With focused intention, we can bring about new realities in our world. The universe reflects to us whatever we choose.

And immediately the arguments begin.

"My child died, and I certainly didn't choose that!"

"If I were creating my life, I'd be rich and happy!"

"I never focused on getting cancer!"

This is why Principle Three needs a fuller discussion than "Change your thinking, change your life." As an evolving species, we have only a glimmer of how this universal law works and how we can work within it. Imagine the earliest humans standing in front of the first fire, saying, "It's pretty and it's warm, but what do we do with it?" That's roughly where we are with the Law of Attraction.

And yet, if we truly have the ability to create our experience on this Earth, think how much more quickly we can evolve! Think of all the good we can do, the healings we can manifest, the peace we can bring about. We don't create perfectly yet—we don't even create well most of the time—but the knowledge that thoughts and feelings determine our reality lifts us to a new level of human awareness. We can begin to make changes as individuals, families, groups, nations and the human race simply by changing our focus of attention.

First, let's explore how the law works. Then we'll look at the common objections.

For centuries, this spiritual law was considered to be about thought. From Proverbs 23:7 ("As a man thinketh in his heart, so is he") to Napoleon Hill's *Think and Grow Rich*, which reintroduced this principle during the Great Depression, the emphasis was on thoughts held in mind.

In recent decades, we have learned that *feeling* has more to do with creating our experience than thought. After all, the Universe does not speak English; it does not need words at all. It operates as a field of energy, and so do we. Imagine yourself as a tuning fork. Your feelings in any given moment set up a vibrational tone. The Universe picks up the tone and hums along, amplifying your sound.

If you are vibrating with joy, you will experience more joy. If you are vibrating with misery, you will experience more misery. Your vibration is reinforced no matter what. Seeing this "evidence" of what we already believe often fools us into thinking the events came first, followed by feelings. We think that something outside of ourselves "made" us happy or sad or angry. But in truth, it's the opposite; we live from the inside out.

For that reason, it's important to focus on the good, focus on what we want, see the glass half full, and stay in a positive energetic vibration. In fact, if we can simply feel happy and positive most of the time, we won't have to bother about treasure maps or make detailed lists of what we want to manifest. We will create everything—or attract; I use the words interchangeably—from a higher consciousness.

This is challenging. Most of us were taught to worry or at least to troubleshoot, to ward off impending difficulties. For that matter, our long-ago ancestors, in order to survive, kept a sharp eye out for the tiger in the woods or the enemy from the next village. The ones who stayed on guard lived long enough to reproduce. We come from a long line of worriers.

Focusing on what we want is never more difficult than when something we don't want has already occurred. The hurdle then not only is to change our thoughts but actually to feel as if the unwanted event is not happening. Or conversely, to feel what we want rather than reacting to what is in the moment.

A thorough explanation of feelings as the key to creation, rather than thoughts alone, comes from Gregg Braden, an author who combines science and spirituality to help explain universal principles to a mainstream audience. In his book *The Divine Matrix*, he acknowledges the difficulty of looking past the appearance of what already exists and focusing instead on what we want:

> If all the do's and don'ts of quantum possibilities are true and emotion is the key to choosing reality, then the question is: How do we feel as if something has happened when the person next to us stares us squarely in the face and says that it hasn't? For example, are we lying to ourselves if we say that a loved one is already healed while we're standing over that person in the intensive care unit of St. Someone's Hospital?

> The irony of this last question is that its very nature eludes any single answer. In a universe of many possible realities, there are numerous potential answers. Somewhere among all those alternate realities there exists a scenario where our loved one's healing has already happened. Someplace there's a reality where the disease never even occurred. For reasons that we may never know or understand, however, this isn't the outcome that's

been awakened—it's not the reality that's lying on the gurney in front of us.

The answer to our question boils down to what we believe about the world and our power to choose. The question then becomes: Which possibility do we pick? Which reality does our loved one or the doctor decide on? To answer this, we must first acknowledge that we have the power to make such a choice.[2]

Therein lies the key: "We must first acknowledge that we have the power to make such a choice." That is not the mainstream view. We are told regularly and ruefully, "You've got to play the hand life deals you." We are only beginning to realize that we are, each of us, the dealer.

The process is not simply to visualize a loved one healthy but to *feel* as if she is already up and walking around. Think it, see it, but most of all *feel* the peace and joy that would come to you from her recovery. When you can feel it, you have turned the corner toward your desire. It's not easy! But this is not a path for spiritual lightweights.

You might say that I advocate living in denial. In a sense, yes. Jesus was talking about this very challenge when he said, "Do not judge by appearances, but judge with right judgment."[3] He could look past the appearance of blindness or leprosy to the whole and healthy person. He could look past the unfairness of his trial and the threats to his life and see the greater good of his ministry.

Years ago, I officiated at the wedding of a couple who had deliberately attracted each other through consciousness. They had each declared to the Universe that they were ready for a major relationship. They knew what they wanted, in that they knew how it would *feel* when they met the right person. But when they met each other, they were a bit alarmed. He was a foot and a half taller and at least a dozen years younger than she was. Their first reaction was: "Not that one!" Gradually, however, they said they recognized each other because the relationship *felt* the way they knew it would. It was what they had wanted all along.

We create in consciousness; however, most of us get the process backwards. We look at what has already materialized, then form opinions about whether we like it or not. The creative process is to focus our thoughts and feelings on what we want in order to choose our future reality from the quantum field. Paying attention to what we *don't* want is useful only long enough to clarify what we *do* want then create it in our experience by shifting focus.

Do we always get to choose what we want? Only for ourselves, not others. If your loved one in the hospital has made a soul choice to leave the Earth, your positive feelings will not keep her alive. But her death could not be in your experience if you were not a match to it in energy and consciousness.

Consider that there is a gift in it for you, some soul lesson or deeper understanding you could not have had otherwise. My friend whose son died at twenty-five is very comforted by the idea that his soul had finished its work here on Earth, and she is open to further spiritual awakening even when brought about by grief.

Human beings, especially in the West, cause themselves untold misery by insisting that death is a tragedy, a failure or an outrage. In fact it is the natural end to a single human lifetime. Souls are always coming and going from Earth, some for short periods and some for long ones. We humans become deeply attached to the physical expression of those souls we love on Earth, and our grief for their deaths is real and justified. But their physical presence is a very limited view of our relationship with them. If they were important in our human experience, they may be soul friends whom we have known for many lifetimes and will see again soon. In consciousness, they are never out of touch, even if they have left the Earth and we have not. Some souls take human bodies for a while, some don't. The love among us does not change.

My personal belief is that we come into human form largely to play with Principle Three, to create our experience through thoughts and feelings. I picture a soul group planning its next human lives from the Other Side, probably swearing that this time we will remember our divine power, this time we will remain in constant contact with God within, this time we will create consciously just what we need and want! Our rediscovery of Principle Three once on Earth reminds us of that intention.

Children still remember they are creators. That's why they are so indignant about not getting everything they want. They arrive on Earth knowing their divine power, but long before they can articulate it, they have been told "No" so often and so firmly that they let go of the belief. Clinging to their understanding that they are the creators of their experience carries too high a price. Those who manage not to forget entirely are blasted for their sense of entitlement.

Which brings us to selfishness.

The Law of Attraction is very often introduced as a gateway to material riches. Face it, the possibility of getting rich commands people's attention. Then the principle is criticized as too materialistic, largely by those who have succumbed to society's dictate that you can't have everything you want and you shouldn't be greedy.

The fact is, you will have whatever you focus on. The law is neutral. We can use it for whatever we might label good or ill, just as we can use gravity to anchor a boat or smash a vase. A universal law does not check our motives or worthiness. It simply exists as law.

Many people dislike the idea of being a creator. They don't want the responsibility for everything that happens in their lives. It's easier to be a victim, to blame others. They are full of examples about events they couldn't possibly have created—a hurricane, a war, a tragedy.

Yet those who work with this law for some time begin to feel empowered. We can decide what we want and tell the universe—"I am healthy," for instance—and it will rearrange itself around our conviction. "Ask and it will be given," Jesus said. The quantum field must take the form of whatever we believe, just as water takes the shape of its container.

"There is a constant, instantaneous calculus taking place with your every thought, word and action," writes Deepak Chopra in *The Third Jesus*. "Most people don't notice good or bad results unless these are dramatic, but the world functions as a mirror down to the minutest detail. The mechanics of consciousness are set up so that inner and outer dimensions match perfectly."[4]

We create not just as individuals but as groups. We are all connected through energy, or the One Mind, and with practice we might begin to change our world. Experiments are springing up via the Internet to gather people who will focus on peace, for instance, or help crops grow where there is famine. We will have much more evidence in the coming years about how best to put Principle Three to work for good in our world. Could we mindfully steer storms away from our shores? Could we lower the crime rate with peaceful thoughts?

Japanese researcher Masaru Emoto published beautiful pictures that he said illustrated the effect of human thoughts on water.[5] Could we clean the planet with our consciousness? Exploring our divine potential is the next frontier for human achievement. We are learning to participate in our own evolution.

Now, even if you have crystal clear intentions and perfect focus, you are creating along with nearly seven billion other human beings who don't necessarily want the same things. We can't possibly bend our human minds around how this works for the highest good of all—we're just ocean waves, remember, not the whole ocean—but the point is that we are only beginning to practice this law and we're not experts yet. Don't be surprised if something shows up that you don't like.

And … don't be surprised if what you initially dislike turns out to be the best thing that ever happened to you. Everyone can tell stories of what seemed to be tragedy turning into a blessing. The universe is biased in our favor, and it answers our deepest, truest desires.

Yes, But I Didn't Create THIS!

Many people love the Law of Attraction as long as they're attracting houses, cars and job promotions into their lives. But they claim an exception when they get sick or experience a loss.

We can't have it both ways.

The universe perfectly mirrors consciousness, and it answers our deepest desires. This is probably the most comforting part of the Law of Attraction. Many people don't trust themselves to create their own lives. They are concerned that ego will dominate or that "stinkin' thinkin'" will lead them astray. Certainly that can happen temporarily. But remember, the universe is responding to vibration, and energy doesn't lie.

Notice your friends who were fired from jobs they hated or who were dumped in relationships that weren't going well anyway. They might have felt rejected in the short run, but they might also have said later they were better off. The universe reflected their deepest desires—to move into a better situation—whether they were aware of it yet or not. Conversely, they attracted exactly what they needed, even when they weren't aware what form it would take.

The same concept helps answer why we sometimes think we are not getting what we want. For instance, you might say you want to be married, but if deep down you fear getting hurt, a mate won't show up. The universe resonates with your deeper desire to stay alone and safe from heartbreak. You may say you want riches, but if deep down you feel unworthy or resent the wealthy, money won't materialize.

You also thwart yourself by yearning and longing or focusing on the lack of what you want. Utilizing Principle Three, your best bet is to go ahead and *feel* as happy and fulfilled as if you were madly in love or wildly rich. So happy that you won't care whether it really happens or not. That's when it will likely happen, because you are a match in consciousness or vibration.

This is how the benevolent universe works in concert with our desires. Consider the estranged family brought together by the illness of a parent. The illness might be the result of the usual fears most humans have about physical breakdown. But the parent's deeper desire might have been reconciliation with his children, and the illness helped bring it about. Indeed, if someone had asked him whether, say, a heart attack would be worth reuniting his family, he might quickly have said yes. At a soul level, he did.

What I find empowering about this idea is that it moves me from victim to creator. It shifts the question. I no longer whine, "Why did this happen to me?" but ask, "Why did this happen *for* me? Where is the gift? Why might I have created or attracted this for my soul's purposes?" Even if the situation is difficult, I can begin to look for the good.

That said, figuring out how or why we created our present experience doesn't matter as much as where we go from here. We create the future by our focus of attention in the present moment, regardless of present circumstances. Knowing this truth, we can ask, "What do I want to create next in my life?" "What is my deepest desire?" It is a lifelong process.

Or perhaps more than one lifetime.

The question of karma is another that can be debated far into the night with no resolution. When the events in our lives seem inexplicable, even for those who believe they create their experience, karma is often the answer they grasp. It must have something to do with a past life, they say.

Maybe, but that doesn't let us off the hook as creators now. As the Hindus teach it, karma is not a system of reward and punishment but a balancing of soul experience. A life of wealth might balance a life in poverty, illness with health, etc. We choose those balancing events for our soul's growth. They are not foisted on us to make us atone for our actions in the past. We are free to make our own decisions at every turn, and each has a consequence.

Yes, But You've Got to Play the Hand Life Deals You

It is certainly true that you have a choice about how to react to the events of life. Practicing that alone is a huge step in spiritual growth.

Principle Three goes further, however, saying you can actually change and influence events with your thoughts and feelings. We don't have to chirp "It's all good" and put up with whatever shows up. We can change it.

Or can we? I believe certain major events in our lives might have been planned in broad strokes before we came. Whereas most of our experiences are created in the present, some events or relationships might be soul contracts, something we agreed to for a specific purpose in this lifetime. It helps me make sense of life.

As I was finishing this chapter, my friends' teenage son leaped to catch a Frisbee one Saturday afternoon and landed crooked, snapping his leg bone and cutting off circulation to his foot. After some frightening emergency surgery that saved his leg, he began his long recovery. Every time I walked into the hospital room and saw this skinny kid on the bed with his exhausted parents beside him, I thought, "This just isn't fair!" What a ridiculous waste of his time and youthful energy.

One day he asked me why he might have created this. He wasn't angry, nor was he blaming himself. He was just curious, wondering why he couldn't sense and avoid this pitfall. His internal guidance system often steered him away from danger, he said, but not this time. I gulped and stammered and have been trying to come up with answers for myself ever since. After all, I keep insisting we are the creators of our own experience, no exceptions.

And I do believe it, regardless of all the people telling me "stuff just happens" or "some things are out of our control," including some spiritual people I respect. They point to hurricanes and tornadoes, fires and floods, the elements of suffering that do not seem to be manmade. But I also know people who believe even natural events are a mass creation, and that fires, floods and earthquakes reflect the consciousness of our troubled planet. I suspect if we could know every detail about how the Law of Attraction works, we would understand the macro and the micro creations. We would see exactly how events are created and exactly why each person did or didn't draw the event into their lives. After all, for all the people caught in traumatic events, many more avoid them.

It's my belief that if the universe reflects consciousness, then there can be no random fate. Either we are a vibrational match to an event or not. If not, we will not rendezvous with it. If so, the reasons we attracted it into our experience are as varied as the individuals.

So what about my young friend in the hospital? Why isn't life perfect for those who already know their power as creators? Maybe we create the imperfections for a reason. Maybe the boy and his parents had a soul contract to experience this together, with benefits for each of them. This is not predestination—our creative abilities are always with us, and we can always change our minds—but this might be an agreement they carried out at the soul level.

One of my favorite spiritual teachers and colleagues, Rev. Ed Townley, believes every person is on a hero's journey. Ed and I quibble regularly about just how easy or difficult life is intended to be.

Joseph Campbell defined the hero's journey as the quintessential tale, the story that humans have been telling in different forms for millennia, a template from the collective unconscious. On the hero's journey, the hero first is called to something greater that takes him or her out of a too-familiar comfort zone. Dorothy is carried from black-and-white Kansas and dropped into the magical Land of Oz. Luke Skywalker leaves the boring sand planet to answer the distress call of Princess Leia. Harry Potter escapes his controlling relatives on Privet Drive for wizard school at Hogwarts. The journey begins.

Along the way, the hero collects allies and enemies. He must overcome fears and discouragement. She learns and grows and finally triumphs, then returns home wiser, richer, more authentic.

The focal point of the hero's journey is always overcoming adversity. My friend Ed maintains there will always be a Wicked Witch of the West blocking our paths, a Darth Vader, a Voldemort. That's the human experience, he says; it's the reason we came to Earth. If we had wanted to live in perfect bliss, we could have stayed on the Other Side in pure positive energy.

I agree that we came into human form as a great adventure, to learn and to play, to explore the wonders of Oz like Dorothy. But we also came to learn how to wield our own power, like Harry Potter, and as we move into the upper grades, we should be able to create more adeptly the lives we want. We outgrow the exploding wands and bring about more harmony.

Because our creations are mixed in a soup with seven billion others at varying levels of consciousness, we are unlikely to create a utopia anytime soon. But I believe the more deliberately we employ Principle Three, the more peaceful and happy our lives will be.

Yes, But What About God's Will for My Life?

This is similar to another common question about the Law of Attraction—where is God in all this? Isn't it uppity to think I can just decide whatever I want and create it?

Back to Principles One and Two. We are never separate from God because we are expressions of the divine. God is not an old man watching from a distance and sending challenges to test us. Spirit is a force of love and creative energy expressing through us, as us.

A great many people believe that our duty as human beings is to discover and surrender to God's will for our lives. Implicit in this belief is the assumption that God demands something contrary to our own desires.

What if it is the other way around? Because we are spiritual beings having a human experience, we have come to Earth with divinely inspired intentions and purposes. Desires spring up as reminders of why we came or as directional signals of where to go next. They are the basis of our power to create.

"Desire" gets a bad rap, so let's define the term.

Desire propels us to want more. It drives all the improvement in our lives and in the world. A baby desires to walk, a teenager desires to drive, an adult desires to marry, have children, work, make the world a better place. Doctors desire to heal, teachers to inspire, police to protect and serve, and on and on. Desires propel us to be better, to contribute, to make meaning in our lives.

In terms of Principle Three, desire is a clue to what we might call God's will. Emilie Cady, a New York City doctor and metaphysician, wrote in her 1903 classic *Lessons in Truth*, "Remember this: Desire in the heart for anything is God's sure promise sent beforehand to indicate that it is yours already in the limitless realm of supply, and whatever you want you can have for the taking."

Whatever we desire is already headed our way, she says. "It is the first approach of the thing itself striking you that makes you desire it or even think of it at all."[6]

Cady is saying our will *is* God's will. It bubbles up from the divine within us. There is no deity watching us and making plans for our lives. If we are one with All That Is, if we are God in human form, how could our wills be separate or different?

We receive guidance when we move closer to who we truly are, when we move into Christ consciousness, and allow divine ideas to flow through us, as us. It's all God. We are simply allowing the desires to come forth, like opening a valve within us. Isn't it wonderful to know we are on the right track, in terms of doing what we call God's will, when we are following our bliss, doing what we love and desire to do?

Even better is that most of our desires will be fulfilled beyond our wildest dreams when we allow the good into our lives. Allowing would seem obvious, but as we've said, sometimes we hold at bay whatever we've attracted by feeling unworthy or focusing on what we lack. It always comes back to consciousness, the thoughts and feelings that dominate our energy.

How can we tell whether we're on the right track or living in alignment with our desires? It feels good. Our emotions are a guidance system to steer us toward our highest and best.[7]

This is not what we were taught. Most of us were told life is a difficult struggle that requires hard work and ends in death. And that whatever we want is likely to be wrong, selfish and unrealistic. What a miserable way to live!

How much better to know that a loving Creator set up a universe in which we get whatever we want by focusing on it. Whatever we desire is available to us. We know we're getting close to it when we feel good.

That is worth surrendering to.

***

"A state of expectancy is a great asset; a state of uncertainty—one moment thinking "perhaps" and the next moment thinking "I don't know"—will never get desired results. Even God can give you nothing until you make up your mind about what you expect."

—Ernest Holmes, *How to Change Your Life*[8]

Meditation

on Principle Three

I am fully divine and fully human, as Jesus was. I am on Earth to express God as me, a part of Spirit in its infinite variations. I am free and unlimited, the creator of my experience. What I believe comes to me. What I want is already mine. What I perceive becomes real. What I know is the playfulness and creativity that I recognize as God's image in me. We are cocreating together, my life, this world, all that is. I play a part, I have a role, and the universe would not be complete without me. The future is mine to design.

Principle Four

**Prayer is creative thinking
that heightens the connection with God-Mind
and therefore brings forth wisdom, healing,
prosperity and everything good.**

In Jesus' Words ...

So I tell you, whatever you ask for in prayer,
believe that you have received it,
and it will be yours.

—Mark 11:24

Your Father knows what you need before you ask him.
—Matthew 6:8

If you abide in me, and my words abide in you,
ask for whatever you wish, and it will be done for you.
My Father is glorified by this, that you bear much
fruit.

—John 15:7-8

Father, I thank you for having heard me.
I knew that you always hear me, but I have said this
for the sake of the crowd standing here,
so that they may believe that you have sent me.
—John 11:41-42

Chapter Four

Communion With God

Prayer would seem to be the simplest and most familiar of spiritual concepts. Even little children understand it. Prayer has been practiced by human beings throughout the ages, in many different forms, addressed to gods of many different names. And yet this is where confusion often sets in regarding the Five Principles.

Consider the first three principles in the context of prayer:

1. God is all there is, everywhere and absolute good. This transcendent God is not an old man watching from a cloud, showering us with blessings or discipline when the mood strikes, but is the field of intelligence, love and creative energy in which we live. We can never be separate from the divine Presence.

2. We are expressions of God, like waves in the ocean, and we are divine at our core. The immanent or personal God is within us.

3. We create our own experience when we focus on something and, consciously or not, draw it forth from a field of limitless possibilities, or God-Mind. In this sense, we are cocreators with God.

If we are already creating whatever shows up, then what is prayer? For that matter, why pray at all?

Prayer puts our belief in the first three principles to the test. It forces us to find new concepts and new language for the divine, our relationship to it, and our role in creation. This is not easy. Many people—even those who understand the Law of Attraction and know that their thoughts manifest in their lives—cling to the idea of God as a daddy who will take care of them. They believe they can petition God for favors, behave well enough to deserve blessings, and be protected from the hardships of life. This belief often rationalizes life's apparent vagaries as a test of faith "sent" by God to build our character. "God won't give you more than you can handle," they assure each other.

But this God cannot be defended. This is the God who "allows" war and starvation, who heals some and not others, who protects the favored few. Watch the news after any natural disaster or violent incident. Those who escaped harm will often credit God with saving them. Does that mean God didn't love the others? They weren't worth saving? This is the caricature of God that turns questioners into atheists, a God that doesn't make sense. This God lets bad things happen to good people and does nothing.

The problem, however, is not with God but with our image of a supreme being whose behavior—by our own description—is arbitrary and only sporadically loving. We humans have assigned these traits to God then spent centuries bemoaning that God is not kinder and more protective. And we have continued to pray for kindness and protection against all evidence.

We've got our theory wrong. God is not the one pulling the strings, making things happen or not happen, keeping us safe or not. We are the ones deciding what shows up in our lives, through our focus, our thoughts, our words and our allowing. We are creating our own experience whether we know it or not.

Praying from the level of a cocreator and tapping into our own divinity to create outcomes can be mind-boggling. This new concept of prayer may require a complete overhaul not only in our understanding of God but in our beliefs about ourselves and who we truly are, as well as why things happen. That has been the work of the first three principles.

"To acknowledge that we ourselves have brought into our world everything less than good and to forgive ourselves for all the blame we have ever attached to God or to others for the sorrows and sufferings that have come to us are very important steps in preparation for prayer," wrote Frances Foulkes in *Effectual Prayer*.[1]

After my ideas about God began to change, my attempts at prayer only distressed me. My spiritual friends assured me that all the answers I sought were within. Bad news! I felt mostly emptiness. I had yet to understand that the power within was more than my personality. I still mistook my ego-self for my Self in its entirety and believed my conscious thoughts were my only source of answers.

I had yet to realize that I had 24/7 access to all the attributes of God. I had no tools at that point for communicating with a higher power except to shut my eyes, say "Dear God" and spell out what I thought should happen. And I had yet to understand the power of the word.

"In the beginning was the Word," the Book of John begins, "and the Word was with God and the Word was God."[2]

The Greek *logos* is translated "word" in the Christian Bible but means much more. The original definition of logos implies the conscious intent behind the spoken word; it connotes the creative power of the thought. Even Merriam-Webster's Dictionary defines logos as "divine wisdom manifest … in the world."

Our words contain their own creative power, just as God's words created the Earth. "Let there be light …"

Prayer is where Spirit meets language. Of course the universe does not need our words; it responds to energetic vibration. Words resonate within *us*; we say them for our own sakes. They clarify our thoughts and intentions. They are the voice by which we call forth what we want from the field of possibilities. When we speak consciously, we release our words as if shooting an arrow at a target. We refrain from saying anything we don't want to see in our lives.

That's what Jesus meant when he said, "Ask and it will be given."[3] Asking is not begging or beseeching, as many of us were taught. It is focusing our thoughts, aiming our intentions. Prayer is the time we take to focus, to align ourselves in oneness with the divine and affirm that whatever we need is already ours. This is affirmative prayer.

Like the other principles, affirmative prayer—declaring that our needs are already fulfilled—sounds presumptuous to any who were taught that humans should grovel before God. We may fear that claiming we attracted whatever shows up in our lives drives God out of the process or fails to acknowledge our gifts and blessings. But remember Principle One: It's all God. Jesus taught us to pray in utter confidence. "Your father knows what you need before you ask him,"[4] he said, and "Whatever you ask for in prayer, believe that you have received it, and it will be yours."[5]

Whatever we need or want already exists for us. It is already ours. We can't get ahead of God.

In affirmative prayer, we are remembering who we truly are as expressions of the eternal life force on Earth, and we are taking time to align our thoughts and feelings with our highest good. We affirm our well-being, that our needs are filled and that there is no lack in the universe. Because the universe senses our vibration, prayer is more than the words we utter between "Dear God" and "Amen." Every thought, every feeling, is a prayer.

And the response is always *yes*.

Now, you probably can cite examples when your prayers seemed not to be answered. You can pinpoint prayer requests that you were later *grateful* did not come to pass, when you believe God saved you from yourself by saying *no*.

Maybe so. Prayer is a very personal activity and, because none of us knows the whole truth about God, we conceive of prayer in many different ways. My personal belief is that prayers are not really "answered" at all because, again, every possibility already exists in the quantum field. This is the universal *yes*. We pull from the field of pure potential according to our vibration or focus. This focus may come from the level of personality, where we want all sorts of whimsical things, or from the soul or higher Self, where our deepest desires and intentions are known.

This is why we so often mislabel the events of our lives. This is why so many people declare—later—that getting fired or having cancer was the best thing that ever happened to them. Their deepest desires were addressed, albeit in some unexpected way.

If prayer seems to go unanswered, it is not a decision by God to deny us what we want. It is one of two things:

1. We are attracting from an unconscious, deeper desire, or
2. We are blocking the answer we want.

The two actually may be the same. For example, my life is full of middle-aged women who swear up and down that they want a man in their lives. They insist they are focused on attracting a man, but in fact, they are focused on lack-of-man. Many of them are quick to add how much trouble a man can be! What is the poor universe to do? Match their stated desire for a man, their vibration of lack, or their fear of being hurt and inconvenienced? They are blocking their own good.

Blocks are made of fear, doubt and feelings of unworthiness. Those seeking more money may not feel they deserve it. Those who want to conceive a baby may doubt that it will ever happen. (That's lack–of-baby. It is often remedied by adoption, which is why so many couples conceive after adopting. With a baby in the house, they are no longer stuck in lack-of-baby consciousness.)[6] Those who want love may fear a broken heart, another divorce or attracting another abuser. Whatever shows up—or doesn't—is not God intervening in our lives but our own process of attracting or blocking what we want. We are, even in prayer, the creators of our own experience.

Affirmative Prayer

The process of affirmative prayer begins with a shift in consciousness, then in words. It is praying from a consciousness of God, from the higher Self that is in constant contact with the divine. Deepak Chopra describes it in his book *The Third Jesus*, which is about the Christ consciousness that dwells in every human being:

> At a deeper level everything is unified and whole. When you ask for anything, the One is asking the One, God is asking God.

And there is always a response. … In this case, "response" doesn't mean a yes or no from God. There is no judge deciding whether you are worthy or not. Those perceptions were born of separation. When Jesus told his followers that God sees and knows everything, he was describing the complete intimacy between the self and the intelligence that pervades the universe. Since you could not exist without being part of that intelligence, praying to God is circular, a feedback loop.[7]

Affirmative prayer simply means to remember that whatever we ask for in prayer is ours already. We affirm its availability. Remember the creative power of words: Never put into words anything you do not want. No matter what is happening in the moment, look past the appearance and speak only about what you want. This is how we focus an intention in our own minds. This is how we call forth any given outcome from the field of possibility.

And good luck trying never to speak a negative word! I know three or four people who really try to do this. They speak only affirmations of what they want, regardless of what's happening in the moment. For a long time, I felt as if I couldn't get a straight answer out of them.

"How are you?"

"Terrific!"

"How's the business?"

"Thriving!"

"How's the family?"

"Wonderful!"

I was annoyed until I realized that I was confusing authenticity with negativity. If they were really my friends, I thought, they would be honest. And if they were honest, they would share some sort of complaint! In the world of conscious creation, that's not a friend, that's a downer on their consciousness and mine. Besides, my friends weren't lying; they were just choosing where to focus their attention.

The Greek and Hebrew words that are translated *ask* in the Christian Bible connote a demand or claim. "Give us this day our daily bread" assumes that our wish will be granted, just as we might say "Please pass the salt" with no doubt the salt will be handed over.[8]

Does this turn God into Santa Claus granting our every whim? No. It makes us cocreators, playing our part in creation. It gives us responsibility for what shows up on our planet and in our lives. It reminds us that we have been entrusted with divine power.

"Prayer is not supplication or begging but a simple asking for that which we know is waiting for us at the hands of our Father and an affirmation of its existence," said Charles Fillmore, who founded the Unity spiritual movement in the late 1800s, on the power of prayer to heal.[9]

The most effective prayer of all might be wordless, a period of silence to align ourselves with All That Is and return to the wholeness that is our true nature. The

Buddhists call it *samadhi*, a place of perfect stillness to make room for inspiration. The Tao te Ching says, "Bide in Silence, and the radiance of the spirit shall come in and make its home."

When Jesus spent time alone, and he often withdrew from the crowds, he presumably realigned his consciousness with the divine so that he could continue to express the Christ, the perfect idea of humankind. Each of us is imbued with the divine, and Jesus said we could do anything he could do. Taking time to remember our divine connection and reaffirm our intentions is as necessary to humans as food and sleep.

Affirmative prayer is not the hope that things will get better but the certainty that they already are better. God is already here. Good is already here. We look past appearances, ignore outer circumstances, and affirm the truth of God in every situation.

These examples of prayer illustrate how affirmative prayer is different:

Typical Prayer

Dear God, please make my friend well. He's having surgery tomorrow. Please make sure the doctors don't make any mistakes and there are no complications. Please let him recover quickly and get back to work so he can take care of his family. Be with his wife, because she's really worried. Amen.

Traditional Prayer

Let us pray for all who suffer and are afflicted in body or in mind;

for the hungry and the homeless, the destitute and the oppressed;

for the sick, the wounded and the crippled;

for those in loneliness, fear and anguish;

for those who face temptation, doubt and despair;

for the sorrowful and the bereaved;

for prisoners and captives, and those in mortal danger;

that God in his mercy will comfort and relieve them, and grant them the knowledge of his love, and stir up in us the will and patience to minister to their needs.[10]

Affirmative Prayer

The healing power of the divine flows through my body. I am health, I am wholeness, I am healed. The healing power of God works through the doctors, nurses and medications. I am restored to my natural state of health. I am grateful for my healthy body and for the gifts of this experience.

The specific words used in affirmative prayer are not as important as the intention to affirm what *already exists*, even when we can't see the results yet, and give thanks for it in advance. (Saying "thank you" for a gift that has been received is merely good manners. Saying "thank you" in advance is faith.) The attitude is completely positive. There is no recitation of the problem and no mention of unwanted outcomes. It's as if we are praying from the other *side* of the problem, where all is well and well-being is assured. We project ourselves into that place of pure, positive energy and pray *from* a consciousness of God, of oneness or alignment. We see the people or situation through the eyes of Source.

We also remember that God is not remote from us. There is no need to address God as something Other, no need for praise or supplication. Instead we become still enough to feel the Presence that is always within and around us and to know the love in which we live.

Prayer is not to solicit God but to solidify us. It is to refresh and realign our minds and hearts with the divine. It is to affirm the Absolute Good of the universe. It is to move from ego to soul, to contact the Christ of our being, and begin to live again from our best selves. We do not beg God for favors but call forth that which is already ours, the abundance of a universe built on love, seeded with intelligence, and responsive to our every thought. Prayer brings about miracles because we are the miraculous expression of the Infinite.

Yes, But What About Surrendering to God?

Surrender is living from the higher Self. It is moving from ego to soul, expressing as the Christ rather than the flawed, frightened personality that is dominant for most of us. Surrender is not giving up ourselves but becoming our best selves, knowing that any desire springing from such a higher level of consciousness will be aligned with our good.

By now, you can see the tremendous responsibility each of us has for our lives. Surrender to God is not abdication, throwing up our hands and saying, "*You* take over!" It is, instead, *being* God. It is living as Jesus did, from an inner well of compassion and equanimity that can carry us through the most difficult challenges.

We do not have to do this alone. Just as Jesus relied on the Presence, so can we. In our prayer time, we may imagine ourselves communing with God, in conversation with Jesus, or listening to our spirit guides, angels or ancestors offering reassurance or advice. Others may rest in the silence of their own hearts. Every person might carry a different picture of his or her connection with the divine, but the act of surrender for anyone is to relinquish the ego enough to learn and grow.

Does the soul path ever require a crucifixion? Yes, if you believe that hard times are necessary for growth. No, if you believe your lessons can be easy and fun, or that experiencing joy is the real reason for taking human form. As always, you will create whatever you expect. As stated in Principle Three, your own desires are the best clues to what is in store for you. Desire is your soul, the divine, calling you higher.

Desire often springs from discomfort. Our most spiritually productive periods may be those in which we are thinking, "There has to be more to life than this!" Our comfort zones become uncomfortable. Divine restlessness propels us to something greater.

The worst place to be stuck—and the place where many of us live our lives—is in the gap between where we are now and where we want to be. It is the gap between *asking* (setting an intention, focusing on what we want) and *allowing* good into our lives. It is starving at a banquet, reaching out to receive our gifts with a closed fist.

Most of us have trouble believing that the limits in our lives are self-imposed. How much easier to tell ourselves that God is disciplining us for some good purpose, saying *no* because we don't deserve it, haven't earned it, or couldn't possibly know what's best for us! The truth is, we live in a universe of unlimited abundance and are entitled to more than we can imagine as soon as we are ready to receive it. The system is biased in our favor, the good far outweighs the bad, and we are showered with every advantage. We can choose to stand under this waterfall of blessings with a thimble or a washtub.

Yes, some people in the world are starving. But watch as country after country pulls itself out of poverty and into abundance. Japan and Germany after World War II. Then much of Asia. Next perhaps Africa. In the three-dimensional, human realm, we may see changes in markets or governments, but the change first occurs in consciousness. Well-being abounds, and more and more people are allowing it into their experience. Problems of war, religious conflict, climate change or caring for the poor will all be solved the same way, first by a shift in consciousness, then by unprecedented cooperation and understanding. If we allow it.

Prayer moves us into a state of allowing and nonresistance. We don't receive an answer to prayer as much as we let the answer into our lives. It is like opening the shades to let the sunshine stream in. The sunlight was always there, but we were blocking it.

God is not watching and deciding whether we deserve good outcomes. "It is the Father's good pleasure to give you the kingdom,"[11] Jesus said, and the kingdom is already among us. We need only open ourselves to it.

Yes, But Why Pray for Others?

If each person is creating his or her own experience, does it make any difference if we pray for them?

It does seem to make a difference. The majority of prayer studies document benefits when prayer is used on behalf of others. And while scientists may argue about the best research methods, most ordinary people believe they have seen prayer work wonders.

Prayer is the energy of our thoughts and feelings, and that energy can be directed toward specific outcomes. It can bolster the intention of the person we are praying for. For instance, if a friend in the hospital has an intention to recover, we can add our energy to the healing process.

On the other hand, if our friend has made a soul choice to leave human form, our prayers won't keep him alive. Ultimately, the outcomes are up to each individual's higher Self.

Think of it this way: You might be ready and willing to help a friend build a boat. You might believe your friend would love having a boat and should handcraft it for the ultimate experience in boat ownership. You love boats. You even have special tools for boat-building and plenty of time to help out. But if your friend doesn't want a boat, your good intentions won't be put to use.

We can't know the highest and best outcomes for other people. Each of us has a highly individualized soul journey while on Earth, based on broad intentions and perhaps the unfinished work of past lifetimes. We cannot know another's journey.

Unfortunately for our loved ones, most of what passes for prayer is projection or worry. We form an opinion of what's best for others—they should get well, live longer, stay married, have a healthy child, get a new job—without having a clue about why they came to Earth. The time spent in prayer is too often focused on the lack of whatever is wanted and the fear it will not be given. "Pleeeeeeze, God" is not a prayer. It is a wail, based in fear and doubt and the assumption that we know what is best for others.

Eric Butterworth, who wrote about prayer in *The Universe Is Calling*, described it this way:

> When you worry about a loved one—
> the child on the way home from school,

the wayward youth who has run off to some commune, the husband with the alcohol problem, the friend in the hospital—you are putting the full weight of your consciousness on the side of their difficulty. … You must heal your concern. You must let go and release your loved one into God's care and keeping. The work to be done is in you, on your consciousness, not in the other person.[12]

The last thing we want to do when praying for others is to blanket them in our fear and anxiety. Saying positive words won't mask a fearful vibration; the universe is not fooled. Just as our affirmative prayers can bolster the intentions of those for whom we pray, our fears can add to theirs at an energetic level. So yes, sometimes it is better not to "pray."

An alternative might be to ask for prayer from someone less emotionally involved in the situation. In fact, the less detail that is offered, the easier it is for the person praying to focus on the highest and best outcome without forming an opinion about what is needed. In church, our prayer team received a very nonspecific list of prayer requests to hold in consciousness for the week. "Ann, healing." "Bob, guidance for a new job." "Kathy, peaceful relationship." It is not necessary to know the person or the circumstances for prayer to be effective. Let others stand in faith for you when you are too upset or scared to rest in divine peace.

***

"Spirit intends you to be a radiating center that will draw to you whatever you need to be well and strong, successful and prosperous."

—Myrtle Fillmore, *Healing Letters*[13]

Meditation

on Principle Four

In the stillness of my heart, I turn to God within. In my heart, I know my oneness with the divine. In my heart, I fear nothing, want nothing, lack nothing. In my heart, I rest in the awareness of God's unyielding presence, and I take pleasure in our communion. My soul is the divine. My higher Self is my access to God, the Christ in me. I am an opening for God on the Earth, and I let divine light and love flow through me into the world. I surrender to this knowing, to this purpose, and to the blessings that flood my being as I allow the flow of Spirit in and through me.

Principal Five

Knowing and understanding the laws of life,
also called Truth, are not enough.
A person must also live the truth
that he or she knows.

In Jesus' Words …

I was hungry and you gave me food. I was thirsty
and you gave me something to drink. I was a stranger
and you welcomed me. I was naked and you gave me
clothing. I was sick and you took care of me.
I was in prison and you visited me …
Just as you did it to one of the least of these
who are members of my family, you did it to me.
—Matthew 25:35-36, 40

The time is fulfilled, and the kingdom of God
has come near; repent and believe in the good news!
—Mark 1:15

Truly I tell you, if you have faith
the size of a mustard seed,
you will say to this mountain,
"Move from here to there" and it will move;
and nothing will be impossible for you.
—Matthew 17:20

Chapter Five
Expressing God

At last, we put principles into action! These teachings would be useless if not practiced in the real world. But notice: Four of the five principles are about shifting consciousness *before* changing behavior. Even the fifth principle says "live the truth," which may or may not mean charging out to save the planet.

The good news is that we cannot *not* live the truth. It is spiritual law; it applies to everyone, all the time. We are the divine in expression, every day. We *are* creating our experience with every thought and feeling. We *are* in prayer without ceasing, communing with an exquisitely responsive universe of abundant good. The goal is to live consciously in that awareness and take action as guided by our inner being, even knowing that we often express imperfectly.

Living the truth is more about *being* than *doing*. It's how we show up for whatever we choose to do, whether we are a business executive, stay-at-home mother, healer, teacher or homeless wanderer. When we are living the truth, any action we take will be from a consciousness of Spirit and oneness, with ego in service to soul.

The Five Principles provide steps to lead us from ego to soul, from living unconsciously to living in awareness of truth. Truth is spiritual law; it is Creation at our service. Our work is to learn how to wield our spiritual tools in the human experience.

The first four principles constitute a handy checklist before taking action.

1. Do I affirm divine intelligence and love in this situation?
2. Do I remember my own divinity and that of others involved?
3. Do I take responsibility for attracting this situation into my experience and know that its outcome *for me* will match my thoughts and feelings about it?
4. Have I aligned myself with God, the universe, the Good, and received guidance before I act?

Any action that feels forced, impulsive or emotional is likely not to be in principle. Acting in principle usually brings a reassuring sense of being on the right track even if others object. It is not stubbornly exerting your will, but it might be moving to the beat of your own drummer or following your own star.

Every time you hear about the Law of Attraction or the principle that we are creating our experience in consciousness, you are likely to hear someone harrumph that you can't just sit around thinking positive thoughts. You have to take action! Actually, no. The shift in consciousness makes the difference, no matter how many résumés you send out, no matter how hard you work, no matter how long your house has been on the market. Life is consciousness first, then we take action as we are inspired.

That said, I understand what people mean when they say: "Act your way into believing" or "Fake it till you make it." Act first, and a change of mind and heart will follow. They believe that action not only is required to make changes but that it brings about the shift in consciousness that is needed.

That logic seems to benefit a lot of people, but I would bet a change of mind has already begun to take place or they would not be willing to take any action. It's true that action can lead to further shifts in consciousness. Eating salad instead of chocolate cake, for instance, helps me stay in a consciousness of good health. But in actuality, my consciousness of health prompted me to choose salad in the first place. Each builds on the other.

Spiritual action does not demand marching in the streets against war, saving the environment, or turning corporations into socially responsible do-gooders, although some people will express truth in that way. It means, at base, integrating our divine essence into ordinary, annoying, daily living with its drudgery, confusion and difficult people. How do we apply these principles when we're sick, broke, heartbroken, scared, angry or apathetic? How do we make choices, day in and day out, in alignment with principle, so that we can—bit by bit—create the kingdom of heaven on earth?

The question is being asked more often. Students of spirituality, psychology, metaphysics and human potential seem eager to move from study into action. But there are no formulas for using principle. Not only is every individual different, but each came to Earth with a different purpose and path. That's why our ability to create our own experience is so useful. We can attract the unique experiences that are perfect for each of us and take action as guided.

My friend Laura Shepard, who has practiced principle for many years, compares each human being to a pot of chicken soup. (This is ironic, considering how rarely Laura cooks, but the metaphor works.) Each pot has a slightly different combination of ingredients and seasonings. One may have more carrots, one more potatoes. One may be flavored with ginger and another with basil. One may need more salt but another needs pepper instead. Consider these ingredients to be the elements of consciousness—beliefs, attitudes, assumptions, histories, hurts, prejudices and soul paths—conscious or not. Every person holds a different mix of consciousness, so each will attract different people and events into life and make different choices for action.

Laura and I have found that even when we have the same goals and cite the same principles, our actions may be different. For example, we both want to be healthy. For me, that means getting regular checkups. Laura avoids doctors whenever possible. She doesn't want to go looking for trouble.

We are both practicing principle. We both believe the universe responds to our energetic vibration. Laura vibrates with health when she assumes everything is okay and ignores any aches and pains. I vibrate with health because I've been tested and cleared. For me, unexplained aches and pains would arouse fear and be more likely to attract illness. For Laura, going through medical tests stirs up resistance that might create illness. Each of us has found what works to keep us vibrating in a consciousness of good health.

Relationships are another area where we reach different conclusions based on principle. When Laura is annoyed by her husband (who, for the record, is a great guy), she takes it on herself to clean up her vibration. Rather than react to someone or something outside herself, she vows to choose how she is going to feel. She says it would be out of principle to ask someone else to change so she can be more comfortable.

I agree with her in theory, but I also think it's possible to negotiate, set boundaries and make requests in a relationship, to appeal to the divine in another person. On the other hand, Laura has been happily married for 20 years, so maybe she's onto something.

The point is that people who are consciously practicing principle might choose different actions. The only guideline is to choose whatever keeps you in positive vibration. How do you know when you're in that vibration? The shorthand answer is this: Good feels good, bad feels bad.[1]

When we do, say or think things that feel good, we are putting ourselves in a positive consciousness and will naturally attract good things. We are in alignment with universal law or principle. We are living from soul rather than ego. It is a feeling of gratitude, contentment and sometimes exhilaration. We feel all is right with the world, no matter the appearance. We are more aware of the divine within us.

When we are making ourselves feel bad—through our words, actions or negative thoughts—then we attract at that lower level. We are probably trapped in ego. Our negative feelings let us know that we are disconnected from principle, the truth, the divine. Bad feels bad.

Action vs. Activism

This is why crusades to change the world so often don't work. A war on drugs or poverty, a fight against crime or terrorism, a battle against cancer or autism, sets up resistance by definition. Energy flows where attention goes, and it may go to the positive or negative side of any issue.

For example, are we marching against war or in favor of peace? The march might look the same—people moving down the street, chanting and holding placards. But the universe reflects the thoughts and feelings that are involved. Angry resistance will be met at some point with angry resistance. Peace begets peace.

Eckhart Tolle, whose book *A New Earth* is a manual for living from the soul instead of ego, cautions that activism often stems from resistance or the collection of personal wounds and baggage that he calls the pain-body:

> Sometimes people with such dense pain-bodies become activists fighting for a cause. The cause may indeed be worthy, and they are sometimes successful at first in getting things done; however, the negative energy that flows into what they say and do and their unconscious need for enemies and conflict tend to generate increasing opposition to their cause. Usually they also end up creating enemies within their own organization, because wherever they go, they find reasons for feeling bad, and so their pain-body continues to find exactly what it is looking for.[2]

The pain-body is ego on the march, or self-will run riot. People who live unconsciously and act from old pain have mistaken their pain-bodies for who they truly are, Tolle says.

No one expects you to radically change the world. Even Jesus didn't overthrow the Roman Empire or establish peace on earth. Mother Teresa didn't eradicate poverty. In fact, she said, "We feel that what we are doing is just a drop in the ocean, but the ocean would be less without that drop."[3] Those remembered as avatars or saints were probably more notable for the different consciousness they held, for their presence and their understanding of the human experience, than for any dramatic accomplishments.

Putting principle into action starts as an inside job. To bring peace to the world, be peaceful. That means not yelling at the kids or making obscene gestures at other drivers. It means patience in the grocery line, even if the person in front of you clearly has more than ten items for express checkout. You don't have to find a solution for the Middle East to contribute peace to the planet. If enough people begin to be peaceful, peace will erupt on Earth just as violence does now.

If you want to practice principle beyond your own home, try seeing the divinity in other people. Try treating each person you meet as a messiah in disguise. Try taking responsibility for what you have created in your life and what your family, your city, country and the human species have created together. Try spending some time alone to remember your connection to Spirit and move ego aside to let the divine flow through you.

Remember that you are moving energy with your consciousness regardless of whether you get off the couch. "Action" includes the thoughts and feelings you contribute to the whole, the One Mind or, as Pierre Teilhard de Chardin called it, the *noosphere*, the thinking layer of Earth.

We know from Principle Three that what we focus on expands. That means we can "live the truth" merely by focusing. Focus on peace and harmony in your workplace. Focus on love in your family. See whether it makes a difference. If nothing else, you are adding peace and love to the One Mind, thought by thought. It adds up.

By the same token, focusing on whatever we dislike empowers it. This explains self-fulfilling prophecies. We predict something bad will happen, and it does. What we focus on grows, whether our focus is positive or negative. The emotional energy packs the wallop, even more than the content of our thoughts.

This is *metaphysics*, which means above or beyond the *physical*. Most of our experiences have elements of both.

For example, leaders are elected physically with our votes but metaphysically through our collective consciousness. Suppose Candidates A and B are running for president of the United States. Half the country is voting for A. The other half not only supports B instead but despises A. The polls say it's a toss-up, but Candidate A will take office because of the tremendous emotional focus on him or her. Both sides are choosing Candidate A with their attention and emotion. Both are providing energetic support for A whether they go into the voting booth or not. Half are creating the outcome they want, while half are creating what they don't want through their fear, resistance and negativity. As we learned in Principle Three, we create both ways, through positive and negative vibration. We create by thought and emotion, or focus and energy.

"Pronounce every experience good and of God," said Charles Fillmore, "and by that mental attitude you will call forth only the good. What seemed error will disappear and only the good will remain. This is the law, and no one can break it."[4]

This is good to know. It means that rather than fighting against whatever we dislike, we can simply withdraw our energy from it and it will leave our experience. Don't like violent movies? Then don't see them, don't talk about them, don't protest them, don't think about them. Pretty soon, you may notice that violent movies are no longer part of your experience. You won't stumble across them on TV, you won't hear about them when they open at the box office. If enough people did this, eventually fewer such movies would be produced. But in the meantime, they will leave *your* experience. It's the same for record lyrics, pornography, polluters and anything else you disapprove of. Simply withdraw your energy.

"But," you argue, "we've got to do something! Even if it doesn't affect me, it affects others, and it has to be stopped. It's bad and wrong, and I would be cold and selfish not to care."

I'm not saying you shouldn't care. I am saying be careful *how* you care. Are you caring through resistance or through support? Are you against something or in favor of its opposite? If you care, envision a clean environment, imagine G-rated song lyrics then, if you are so guided, support decisions to make them so. Support them with your consumer spending, even support them by lobbying. Just don't mistake resistance for support. Make sure any action comes from an energy of what you are *for*. It can be tricky because you may be surrounded by people who are energized by their resistance. But acting from positive vibration will feel better and have more lasting effects.

Picture this: You are at a buffet table laden with food. Some of it you like and some of it you don't. Would you throw a tantrum about the food you don't like, insisting that it be removed? Would you condemn the people who enjoy that particular dish? Or would you simply focus on what you do like and ignore the rest?[5]

In some cases, to "live the truth" may not require taking physical action, only metaphysical action. The metaphysical is more powerful, after all. An energy shift always precedes physical changes. The fall of the Berlin Wall in 1989 was the result of a shift in collective consciousness. The green movement to save the environment is the result of collective consciousness. When enough people begin to think a certain way, when we reach a tipping point in awareness, then outward, physical change begins to happen. That's how we create as a group. Economists even measure group consciousness; it's called the Consumer Confidence Index. When consumers are positive about the economy, it thrives. When they become fearful, we slide into recession.

Yes, we create the bad stuff as a group too. If a personal illness can be the result of fear or resistance, so can an epidemic. If personal anger can turn violent, so can the collection of human grievances. Events are physical and metaphysical. The terrorist attacks of September 11, 2001, were, physically, the decision of a small group to attack the United States. Metaphysically, they reflected the human consciousness of violence; a world awash in anger, fear and resistance; and the widespread belief that problems are solved by killing the perceived perpetrators.

Hence the term: mass consciousness. When beliefs or attitudes are held by nearly everyone, they will inevitably erupt into the physical world just as a volcano releases the energy pent up below the Earth's surface. We may take turns claiming the roles of perpetrators and victims, but we are all participating in the creation.

Living the truth, or practicing principle, is very often a swim upstream against mass consciousness. It is staying healthy despite the bombardment of television commercials about disease. It is feeling prosperous no matter what the economic news. It is staying active regardless of society's expectations for aging. It is loving others despite daily examples of inhumanity. Living the truth we know—that every person, place or thing is an expression of God the Good and that we create our own experience—flies in the face of mass consciousness. But doesn't it feel better than fear, than guarding against hurt and expecting the worst, better than living as a helpless victim of fate?

Into Service

Some people discover that taking action based in principle requires them to upend their lives. They decide over time to change jobs, cities, friends, spouses or lifestyles. Others continue to live quietly but more deeply as they become aware of the laws at work in their lives. Putting principles into action, or living the truth, may or may not mean making outward changes.

What often happens is that people who are living in principle notice their cups overflowing and want to give from their abundance. They do not take action as much as they provide service. They see what needs to be done and begin to do it, often unnoticed and unsung. They are not out to right wrongs or change the system as much as to pitch in, to do what they can to help in an imperfect world.

This happens naturally when we see the oneness in all beings, when we know ourselves to be expressions of Spirit, when we are confident of attracting whatever we need, and when we are in conscious contact with the divine—in other words, when we are living the first four principles. Service is the next natural step. We were never islands unto ourselves, and we cannot behave as if we are.

"Power in life, in earth and in heaven, lies in ability to minister," wrote Imelda Octavia Shanklin in *What Are You?* "Service is coordination with the laws of being. It is the law of heaven."[6]

This type of action is ancient spiritual practice that permeates most religions. The Jews speak of *tikkun alam*, which means "healing and repairing the world." Muslims donate at least 2.5 percent of their wealth to help the poor; charity is a pillar of Islam. My friend Bhante Y. Wimala, a Buddhist monk, sets up medical camps in Kenya and worked on tsunami recovery in his home of Sri Lanka. He gives wheelchairs to the disabled in Africa and helped bury the dead after a devastating cyclone in Myanmar. A lifetime of meditation led him into inspired action.

Service is not subservience, nor a chore to be dispatched. It is the divine in us touching the divine in another. Yes, others have created their own experiences, and a shift in consciousness might benefit them. Yes, the poor will always be with us. If we could see through the eyes of Source, we would know that everyone is creating, learning and expressing perfectly. But down here in our three-dimensional, human world where people suffer, we can tend to each other's physical needs.

Turn on the news. You will find no end of opportunities to serve others.

Yes, But All the News Is Negative

Your goal is to stay in a positive vibration so that you are always attracting from a consciousness of well-being. You might decide to limit contact with the outside world for a while, but the goal is to hold the high watch regardless of what is going on around you.

Try an experiment: Watch the news for five minutes while thinking, "We're all doomed. The world is going to hell in a handbasket." Notice how you feel and what's on the news. Then watch another five minutes while thinking, "The world is an awesome place." Notice how you feel.[7]

Where is the negativity? Is it in the information itself or in the attitude and assumptions with which you receive it?

We see the world through our own filters. *Filters* is another word for consciousness. Nothing enters or leaves our experience without being sifted through the filters of our beliefs, assumptions and histories. What if we could remove them on occasion, rise above them?

Jesus suggested that we be in the world, not of it. That's another way to say we can live from soul and not ego, expressing the Christ, the divine within each of us, even in our human form. Checking out completely—turning off the news, turning our backs on our fellow humans—doesn't help anyone. But neither does immersing ourselves in hysteria. We know by now that living in fear and anger is the worst possible consciousness from which to create the world we want.

So, some thoughts about the news from a former reporter (me):

- News by definition is what's unusual and out of the ordinary. It is not intended to reflect typical human existence. If a million children get up, go to school, come home, do their homework and go to bed, it's not news. It's routine. If one child takes a gun to school and opens fire, it's news. When I worked as a reporter in one major city with a high crime rate, we didn't bother to cover murders unless several people were slain together. Be grateful if you live in a place where murder is still news. You don't want it to become routine.

- The world is heavily tilted toward our well-being. If the news truly reflected the human condition, it would be good news or at least neutral news about 23.99 hours a day, with only a blip of the bad. Keep the news in perspective. Notice the well-being in your own life. Most of what you see on the news is not happening to you. Remember you have the power to create whatever you want in your life regardless of outer circumstances.

- The news reflects eruptions of mass consciousness. If it is heavily weighted with violence and death, consider what that says about the thoughts and feelings we hold as a society. Change starts within. Let there be peace on Earth, and let it begin with me.

- Try watching the news with Principles Four and Five in mind, prayer and action. Bless those involved, send them positive, loving energy. Then pray: *What is mine to do?* or *Show me my perfect place of service.* Ask for guidance and wait to see whether you feel called to take action. Eventually you will know— from the urgings of the divine within you, from an inner voice as familiar as a friend's—whether to get off the couch and do something.

Yes, But Faith Without Works Is Dead

Action comes naturally to some people and not to others. I have a tendency to think about taking action, but I want to read another book or attend another workshop before I get moving. Still, I believe the universe waits for us to make the first move, then it rushes to support our endeavors.

Jesus didn't sit on a mountaintop and wait for people to come to him for wisdom; he walked all over Israel to teach and heal. He also took breaks to realign his consciousness with the universe, God, the One, before he resumed action.

All people are different. The action you are inspired to take may be more or less than that taken by someone else. Let's say two people are holding a consciousness of attracting a great job. One sends out ten résumés, but the other feels lazy sending fewer than a hundred. Do what feels right for you. Do what keeps you in a positive vibration.

People experiment with this in different ways. I know one couple who began to tithe ten percent of the money they wanted their business to make in the coming year, and their income rose to meet it. One woman packed for a cruise before she had any idea how she would afford to go, but a last-minute cancellation got her onboard. Another friend began getting dressed every morning and driving to the office where she wanted to work. They each took action to demonstrate their belief in the abundance of the universe.

And yet a woman in my church said she increased her business without changing anything except her beliefs about prosperity. The action was purely metaphysical, in consciousness.

God does not require a demonstration of faith, but we make room for our good by opening our minds to receive. If it helps, we can begin to act as if it were already ours. Take any action that helps align your vibration with your desires. Close the gap between where you are and where you want to be. Feel it first, then watch it transpire.

Living the truth will take as many forms as there are people on Earth. Some will look very busy taking action and some won't. What truly matters is what's going on in their hearts and minds, and you can never tell by looking.

Each of us is creating for ourselves, according to our souls' paths, our levels of awareness, and our inspired action. Our vibrations—every thought and feeling—contribute to the One Mind, which means every thought and feeling becomes part of the whole, forever. It all matters.

***

Do not merely listen to the word, and
so deceive yourselves. Do what it says.
—James 1:22

Whatever you have learned or received or
heard from me, or seen in me—put it into practice. And the God of peace will be with you.
—Philippians 4:9

Meditation

on Principle Five

What is mine to do? How am I to serve? I have
come to this human experience not just for myself but
for others, and I stand ready to share God's love with
them. That love expresses through me and as me. I make
myself ready. I ask for my perfect place of service. I live
the truth, knowing that God is all, that I am God, that
we are cocreators, and that I am never separate from
divine radiance. I let my light shine to illuminate those
in darkness. I let my heart expand for those who need
love. I give as it has been given to me, and I am grateful
for us all.

5 Basic Unity Principles–

Adapted for Children and Teens

1. God is all good and active in everything, everywhere.
2. I am naturally good because God's divinity is in me and in everyone.
3. I create my experiences by what I choose to think and what I feel and believe.
4. Through affirmative prayer and meditation, I connect with God and bring out the good in my life.
5. I do and give my best by living the Truth I know. I make a difference!

Acknowledgements

I wonder sometimes how my life might be different had I not met certain people exactly when I did. They have pushed, questioned, cheered and supported me on my path. They have believed in me when I didn't and are never surprised when I succeed.

Laura Shepard offers the kind of complete friendship that women sometimes have. We talk about everything from hair and nails to God to work to relationships to spiritual principle. Laura introduced me to the Abraham-Hicks material, which has shaped my theology and ministry ever since. I was already an ordained Unity minister and thought I knew all about the power of thought to create in our lives. Unity has been teaching it for 120 years. But Abraham restated the Law of Attraction for me in such clear, powerful, up-to-date, pragmatic ways that I have been using ideas, phrases and metaphors from Abraham ever since. Fans of Jerry and Esther Hicks will recognize Abrahamisms in this book, so many that I can't even credit each idea that Abraham has influenced. Laura combed the chapter on the Law of Attraction (Principle Three) with her absolutist view that we are creators of our own experience and, very nicely, let me know that I still don't have it quite right. Probably not. I believe the human race is only beginning to learn how spiritual principles work, and I hope the readers will find practical application that works for them.

Mark Youngblood is another friend whose influence on my thinking has been so pervasive that I could never footnote every idea or phrase that came from him. Mark taught me about subtle energy and how a clear energy field allows me to connect much more easily with my higher Self and create more quickly in my experience. Together we have facilitated weekend workshops about moving from ego to soul using *A New Earth* by Eckhart Tolle, for whom I am also grateful.

Ed Townley is a Unity minister whose primary message is about living from the Christ of our being, the divine within, and creating the kingdom of heaven on earth (Principle Two). He sees the human experience as a hero's journey, and he continues to be one of my great teachers.

In the early days, E.J. Niles and Dianne Camp, both Unity ministers, encouraged my tentative steps onto a new spiritual path even as I worried that I might be struck by lightning. E.J. introduced me to the work of John Shelby Spong, the now-retired Episcopal bishop whose books have shaped much of my theology and understanding of the Bible and who, with his wife Christine, has become a treasured and supportive friend. Dianne gave me permission to question everything, even God.

Coming from a childhood church where questions were condemned as a lack of faith, I appreciate the freedom Dianne encouraged, even as my questioning continues.

Many others—friends, congregants, authors, teachers—have a voice in this book. If any of you believe a phrase originated with you, it probably did. You have given much, shared your divine ideas, and watched patiently as it all gestated in me and emerged as light. I am forever grateful.

Ellen Debenport
Dallas, Texas
Christmas Day, 2008

NOTES

CHAPTER ONE

[1] Charles Fillmore, (1924, November). Untitled and unpublished lesson presented at the Tuesday morning service at Ninth and Tracy, Kansas City, Missouri. Unity Library and Archives, Unity Village, Missouri. (Thanks to Kelly Isola for sharing this reference.)

[2] James Gaither, *The Essential Charles Fillmore*, Unity House, 1999.

[3] John Shelby Spong, *Jesus for the Non-Religious*, Harper San Francisco, 2007.

[4] Acts 17:28 NIV.

[5] John 15:5 NIV.

[6] James Gaither, *The Essential Charles Fillmore*, Unity House, 1999.

[7] Joseph Conrad, *Under Western Eyes*, Penguin, originally published 1911.

[8] Job 3:24 NIV.

[9] Venice Bloodworth, *Key to Yourself*, DeVorss, 1952.

[10] Rainier Maria Rilke, *Letters to a Young Poet*, New World Library, 2000.

CHAPTER TWO

[1] Eric Butterworth, *The Universe Is Calling*, Harper San Francisco, 1993.

[2] Matthew 5:14 NRSV.

[3] Matthew 17:17 NRSV.

[4] Luke 23:34 NRSV.

[5] Bill Cosby as quoted in *The Atlantic*, "This Is How We Lost to the White Man," by Ta-Nehisi Coates, May 2008.

[6] John 14:6 NRSV.

[7] Alfred Lord Tennyson, "The Higher Pantheism," 1869.

[8] Michael Dowd, *Thank God for Evolution*, Council Oaks Books, 2007. (See this text for much more on brain science in a spiritual context.)

[9] Ibid.

[10] From a statement to be signed by chaplain employees of Marketplace Chaplains USA, based in Dallas, Texas.

[11] Eckhart Tolle, *A New Earth*, Dutton, 2005.

[12] Col 1:27 NRSV.

[13] Neale Donald Walsch, *The Little Soul and the Sun*, Hampton Roads, 1998.

[14] Elisabet Sahtouris, *EarthDance: Living Systems in Evolution*, iUniversity Press, 2000.

[15] *Gospel of Thomas*, Saying 3, translated by Thomas O. Lambdin, <theologywebsite.com>

CHAPTER THREE

[1] *The Dhammapada,* No. 1, translated from the Pali by F. Max Müller, Oxford: Clarendon Press, 1881.

[2] Gregg Braden, *The Divine Matrix*, Hay House, 2007.

[3] John 7:24 NRSV.

[4] Deepak Chopra, *The Third Jesus: The Christ We Cannot Ignore*, copyright © 2008 by Deepak Chopra. Published by Harmony Books, a division of Random House, Inc.

[5] Masaru Emoto and David Thayne, *The Hidden Messages in Water*, Beyond Words Publishing, 2004.

[6] H. Emilie Cady, *Lessons in Truth,* Unity House, 1941.

[7] For much more on allowing and the emotional guidance system, consult any of the books and recordings from Abraham by Jerry and Esther Hicks.

[8] Ernest Holmes, *How to Change Your Life*, Science of Mind Publishing, 1982.

CHAPTER FOUR

[1] Frances Foulkes, *Effectual Prayer,* Unity House, 1945.

[2] John 1:1 NRSV.

[3] Matthew 7:7 NRSV.

[4] Matthew 6:8 NRSV.

[5] Mark 11:24 NRSV.

[6] Gregg Braden, *The Divine Matrix*, Hay House, 2007.

[7] Deepak Chopra, *The Third Jesus: The Christ We Cannot Ignore*, copyright © 2008 by Deepak Chopra. Published by Harmony Books, a division of Random House, Inc.

[8] Eric Butterworth, *The Universe Is Calling*, Harper San Francisco 1993.

[9] James Gaither, *The Essential Charles Fillmore*, Unity House, 1999, from "The Omnipotence of Prayer" (1939).

[10] *The Book of Common Prayer*, Seabury Press.

[11] Luke 12:32 NRSV.

[12] Eric Butterworth, *The Universe Is Calling*, Harper San Francisco, 1993.

[13] Myrtle Fillmore, *Myrtle Fillmore's Healing Letters*, Unity House, 1954.

CHAPTER FIVE

[1] Thanks to Abraham-Hicks for this expression.

[2] Eckhart Tolle, *A New Earth*, Dutton, 2005.

[3] Mother Teresa, *A Simple Path*, Ballantine Books, 1995.

[4] Charles Fillmore, *Talks on Truth*, Unity House, 1926.

[5] Thanks to Abraham-Hicks for the example.

[6] Imelda Octavia Shanklin, *What Are You?*, Unity House, 1929.

[7] Thanks to Scott DeGraffenreid of N2 Millennials for this exercise.

About the Author:

Ellen Debenport has served as senior minister to Unity churches in Dallas and Wimberley, Texas. Debenport has a bachelor's degree in journalism from Baylor University and worked as a reporter for United Press International and the *St. Petersburg Times* before becoming a minister.

www.ellendebenport.com

B0054